TOWER OF BABEL
Speculations on the Cinema

^

TOWER OF BABEL

Speculations on the Cinema

ERIC RHODE

CHILTON BOOKS
A Division of Chilton Company
PUBLISHERS
Philadelphia and New York

Published in the United States of America, 1967, by Chilton Company

Library of Congress Card Number 67-12294

Printed in Great Britain

To My Mother and Father

Contents

INTRODUCTION   9

Jean Vigo   17

Robert Bresson   35

Sergei Eisenstein   51

Humphrey Jennings   67

Fritz Lang (The German Period: 1919–33)   85

Jacques Rivette   109

Federico Fellini   121

Alain Resnais   137

Max Ophuls   159

Andrzej Wajda   171

Satyajit Ray   191

INDEX   209

Acknowledgements

I am deeply grateful to M. J. Lasky, editor of *Encounter*, for having suggested I should write a book on the cinema and for having encouraged me in this project; to the Congress of Cultural Freedom, for a generous grant which made such a project possible; to Stanley Reed, Director of the British Film Institute, and Ernest Lindgren, Curator of the Archive, for allowing me to use many of the Institute's facilities; and to many of my friends at the Institute, most notably Peter Harcourt and Sue Bennett, for helping me patiently in all sorts of ways. I am indebted also to my editor at Weidenfeld and Nicolson, Edward Victor, for the great care he has taken over the book. Finally, I would like to thank Penelope Houston on two counts: for having made a number of invaluable comments on my typescript; and for having published some of my first adventures into film criticism in *Sight and Sound*.

I need hardly add, though, that all errors of fact, or follies of judgement, must be laid squarely on my head.

London,　　　　　　　　　　　　　　　　　　　　　E.R.
November, 1965

Introduction

What is this book about? I could argue grandly that it is concerned with the way in which a director's insights relate (or fail to relate) to his more generalized view of society and politics; with how he sees things and how he would *like* to see them; with the often fruitful clash between temperament and ideology.

But putting the case so abruptly makes it sound too Olympian. It gives the pleasant but false impression that one critic at least knows all the answers, can provide rules of thumb, a manual for the tyro director. Nothing is further from the truth. In fact, my aim in taking on this project was much simpler. I was fascinated by the work of a number of directors and I wanted to come to terms with them; I wanted to learn why I was either attracted to, or angered by their films. The business of film-going can be compared to a dialogue with people we care about. The discussion may often be affectionate, occasionally heated; but – no question – it should never be impersonal, never indifferent. For films are not made or seen in a void. If the cinema is an art (and I believe it is), then it demands a total participation from both its artists and its critics, a total saturation of the self. It calls on our feelings and intellect, sensibility and judgement, high seriousness and low humour – in fact, everything.

And yet, you may argue, how dare I hold a director responsible for a film when films are usually made by a group of people? In theory, I have no justification. But as we watch a masterpiece, how irrelevant this argument seems, how remote from our feelings. We are aware of a conviction and a style – aware of having embarked on a direct and quite personal affair;

9

sometimes to settle accounts, at other times to show our gratitude. Art is always a matter for individuals, and once it loses
this basis it founders and sinks into compromise – as in the case
of a director shackled by studio directives, or a critic dragooned
by a Press (or Party) line.

My point of departure, then, was the act of sharing a director's vision. And yet, as I explored my memory of this experience
I found myself being snarled up again and again by the thorny
problem of the particular and the general. How does this vision
take shape, how does it take on the force of a persuasion about
society and politics, how does it inform a plot? Such questions
nagged at me in such a way that it would be fair to claim that in
writing this book I discovered not so much a central theme as
a central obsession.

Still, I *have* tried to protect myself from the charge that I
value someone's work either by his stated intentions or, purely,
by my own response. Ezra Pound once wrote that he judged a
man's sincerity by his technique – a salutary reminder. In the
main, my arguments are also based on the assumption that
once a director decides on a technique he commits himself to
certain social and political attitudes. But what is meant by a
technique? Quite simply, the method by which an artist orders
or reveals his experience; the choice of things he includes in
his work and (just as important) the sort of things he excludes.
A technique will soon expose its scope and limitations; so that
a bad one, for instance, will soon condemn itself on internal
evidence, and – by implication – reflect adversely on the politics
of its creator. As I try to show in the chapter on Eisenstein,
authoritarian beliefs tend to lead to a too rigid and impoverished technique. I have found it more useful, though, to trouble
myself over the ways in which this technique may be too rigid
and impoverished, rather than to try and make a political
judgement based, say, on some remark thrown out by the
director. After all, the least effective method of proving whether
a banknote is forged or not is by questioning its alleged engraver.

An example from one of the pioneers illustrates this approach.

In the second half of *The Birth of a Nation* (1915), D. W. Griffith employs a considerable number of rhetorical tricks to defend the practice of slavery; for instance, he shows the Negro as a savage who, given the chance, will oppress the white man and rape his wife. The case is put so strongly that we are even induced to cheer on the last minute arrival of the Ku Klux Klan – a remarkable feat. This rhetoric is so crude, in fact, that we are likely to forget that Griffith had an extraordinary gift for evoking moments of affection; the sort of moments which we usually remember for the rest of our lives, but which mean almost nothing to other people. Lilian Gish kisses a dove and looks with flirtatious irony at her lover – a ridiculous, fragile and charming incident that loses most of its force in the telling. Yet Griffith is able to convey such a force. The cinema is a fraternal activity, and when a director is able to share his pleasure in the world with us we begin to find the germ of a commitment.

What happens, then, when Griffith moves on from the particular to the general, when he deals with those social and political themes of which he was so fond? Technique, and not prejudice, may give us a clue. *The Birth of a Nation* ends, quite literally, in the clouds – as angels swirl around, and men of all nations meet on equal terms. At other times, intolerance (when disapproved of) is shown in an allegorical form. I don't believe this theatricality can be ascribed solely to the conventions of the period. Its crudity of technique warns us, rather, that Griffith is working at some remove from his creative feelings (and creativity is bound up with generosity). As he abandons his concern for factual truth, his technique slackens; the rhetoric of propaganda takes over, and spite is free to express itself unchecked.

However, I am not arguing that temperament is a negative attribute – that, as T. S. Eliot put it, 'only those who have personality and emotion know what it means to escape from these things.' On the contrary, I believe it is the transmuting nature of a director's temperament that can transform an

11

ideology into a work of art. To think of Vigo as an anarchist, Bresson as a Roman Catholic, or Wajda as a Marxist may take us some of the way towards understanding the assumptions underlying their work, but after a certain point such labels act as blinkers. What I am interested in is *not* the director's conscious ideological attitude, but the attitude that arises from the arduous process of making a film – an attitude generated by the act of playing image against sound, which may be quite different from what he intended it to be. Temperament is inseparably bound up with talent, and without it no ideology whatsoever can redeem the quality of a film.

But by what trick or fluke does temperament coalesce with ideology, so that they flower into art? I am not certain; the activity is so obscure. All the same, there are directors who work closely enough to this creative fusion to give us some inkling of how it takes place. Antonioni is a prime example. I feel it relevant that his talent should be compulsive, that to witness one of his films is to be drawn into a hypnotic world of the imagination. Best of all, the shock of his style is most felt if we come to the film when it is already under way. We leave the grey streets and enter the darkened auditorium: before us is a sequence of images whose logic is quite independent of the usual narrative conventions of the cinema; the editing and composing of shots is as disturbing as the signature at the end of a long letter in typescript. Yet within moments I, at least, find myself enthralled by this style. I begin to lose sight of its oddity and begin to accept its vision as natural. A compulsive art is irrational: and after the viewing is over and we are once more submerged by the grey streets we may question Antonioni's views on the failure of communication and find them unconvincing. Some critics, in fact, have gone on to argue from this that Antonioni is no thinker and has little to say of importance; yet this claim has scant relevance to the experience we have undergone. What we have seen is the work of a totally committed man – a man struggling to understand the world about him, and bringing a profound seriousness to this task. The style is

12

not imposed on a theme, but arises out of an artist's struggle to understand his subject, and his ability to project this struggle. Without a temperament capable of carrying out this labour, a temperament that refuses compromise or complicity, this style would never have come into being. I am reminded of a Cézanne or a Giacometti, and their ceaseless endeavour to make sense of the motif before them so as to give it life in art.

I think it no coincidence that most of the people I am writing about find it difficult to relate their particular insights to some coherent view of society; so that, though they may describe, quite wonderfully, the relationships of a small group, they seldom extend beyond this group into giving us a Tolstoyian panorama of how these groups relate to each other, and eventually to the whole public realm. As I try to show, the types of withdrawal are numerous: they can take the form of a retreat into stoicism (or 'coolness'), into fantasy, allegory or baseless propaganda. Admittedly, this retreat is more than understandable; urban life in our time has become so complex that it is highly probable no film-maker has the technique to describe it. In *The Human Condition*, Hannah Arendt demonstrated how the notion of the Greek *polis*, in which man was able to realize himself openly in word or deed, has now almost withered away. For the most part, modern politics devotes itself to the problem of social house-keeping. It has become a congerie of private and frequently concealed worlds, in which men (as often as not) are controlled by 'invisible' processes.

The director has every reason to feel baffled by this situation. It is fair, then, that he should sometimes wish to approach it obliquely and to draw inspiration less from a factual knowledge of his society than from a vague reaction to it, at times from a barely defined sense of anguish or menace. I have found again and again that two idealized (and occasionally fantasticated) images are held to contain these sensations, both of them taking the shape of locations: the prison and the city. For obvious reasons, the image of the prison has haunted the contemporary imagination. We live in the age of concentration camps and of

13

ruthless political imprisonment. Also, we are more sensitive to the plight of those confined people society once tended to abandon; the criminal or insane person is no longer treated as being of a race apart. And modern technology (in spite of its splendour) is liable to enhance our fears of incarceration. The rectangular, enclosing shape is everywhere about us – in our apartments, our cars and our buildings. In fact, the city image easily merges and blurs into our image of the prison: both of them stir in us a fatiguing awareness of our loneliness and isolation, of life as a series of cells from which death is the only escape. Adrian Stokes, the writer on aesthetics, has argued that the psychopath is the natural inhabitant of the city since his schizoid tendencies are confirmed by its brutal architecture; and, certainly, it appears appropriate from more than a historical viewpoint that gangster films should usually be played out in the gloom of the asphalt jungle.* The modern city is the perfect image for a society devoid of politics, where events are more conditioned by processes than by actions. At times of despair we might be ironically tempted to agree with Le Corbusier that 'the great city determines everything'.

---

* 'What figure today aesthetically best suits our streets, what figure aesthetically is best framed by our doorways? The answer is the man in a long overcoat with hand within pocket holding a revolver on which his fingers tighten.' Adrian Stokes, *Colour and Form* (1937).

Jean Vigo

Few sequences are more typical of Vigo's style than the opening to *Zéro de Conduite* (1933). An ape-like schoolboy in uniform, seated in a railway carriage, is travelling back to boarding school. The compartment is constricted, filthy and unadorned; smoke billows outside the window; agitated music conveys movement; a passenger sleeps in a corner. The train stops – and our sense of imprisonment is reinforced by a shot, taken from outside, of the boy at the compartment window, low-lit, his hands pressed against the glass. But the boy is impassive, and the shot is brief and unsentimental; going to school or being imprisoned, it seems, is a natural event . . . He is joined by a companion, and the train moves on. The boys play games – make rabbit shadows, rib each other. Two balloons are blown up, and – shades of Apollinaire – stroked as though they were breasts. Plutocratic cigars emerge. Then a low-angled, fantastic, lyrical shot: of smoke outside the carriage and of smoke within, of the boys with cigars in their mouths, a balloon floating above their heads. But, again, the mood is only held for an instant. The train stops abruptly; the sleeping passenger clatters to the floor. 'Il est mort', shouts one of the boys. They push open the compartment door and leap out on to the platform. On the door window we read *Non Fumeurs*.

'If we must be prisoners, at least let us choose our own prison and create there pleasure and joy so that we'll want to live there all our lives.' Vigo cut this Dickensian remark from the final shooting script of *Zéro de Conduite* – perhaps because it stated his feelings too directly. Certainly the notion that man thrives on limitations is at the heart of his work. Vigo assumes that seeds are most likely to burgeon in stony ground, much as he was stimulated by working under difficult conditions on an impossibly low budget. Fantasy, the faculty of improvisation, needs its prison, whether this prison takes the form of a barge or a boarding school or a train. And fantasy seems to transform this prison – seems, as it were, to explode it.

Vigo's critics divide, rather neatly, into two camps: those who stress the prison aspect of his work, and those who emphasize its fantasy. When *Zéro de Conduite* was first shown, the press was hostile almost to a man and found it sordid, hateful, violent, scatological, etc. The trouble was, they confounded subject matter with treatment, and assumed the film to be as squalid as its location. But Vigo's few admirers were as much confused as his denigrators; they became sentimental about his prisons and misunderstood how fantasy transforms rather than destroys them. Vaguely they knew something about Vigo's anarchism, and from it they deduced, falsely, that his aims were subversive. Some of his enemies came to the same conclusion, but for different motives. The French Government, for instance, banned *Zéro de Conduite* for over twenty years on the ground that it endangered national security.

Later critics, however, tended to stress the fantasy aspect of Vigo's films, seeing them as surrealist; since 1945, these critics have made much of his lyricism, his 'delicious poetry'. Now Vigo, it is true, did start to make films at a time when surrealism was a major force – *À Propos de Nice* was made in 1929, the year of the second Surrealist Manifesto; and he did give an enthusiastic lecture on Buñuel's *Le Chien Andalou* (script by Salvador Dali). All the same, to label his work as anarchist and surrealist, and to go no further, is liable to blind us to its unusual merit.

Still, these labels are inescapable. Take anarchism, for instance: the censors were understandably cautious about Vigo from the start, if only because of his father's reputation. The story is beautifully told in P. E. Salès Gomès' biography.* When still in his teens, Eugène Bonaventure de Vigo was arrested on a false charge of theft and jailed for two months. He came out of prison a convinced anarchist and adopted the fighting name of Almereyda (an anagram of *y a (de) la merde*). A short time later, when working as a photographer's assistant, he was again arrested – for carrying a small box of photographic magnesium. The official court chemist described this powder as being an unknown explosive of devastating power. Almereyda was sentenced to a year in jail, much of which time he spent in solitary confinement.

When he was released, he began to edit an anarchist paper; and in 1905 his mistress Emily gave birth to Jean. A painter friend of the family described the child as son of 'undernourished parents (living) in a dirty little attic full of half-starved cats'. The parents were ruining their health with over-work, and Almereyda was continually in and out of jail (mostly in). His son was often brought to visit him.

By 1913 Almereyda and a colleague, Merle, started a new paper, *Le Bonnet Rouge*, and their fortunes began to improve somewhat murkily. War broke out and the paper took up a pacifist line. Almereyda was probably encouraged: he received, it seems, a secret grant from the dubious Malvy, Minister of the Interior, and from a certain Duval who made secret visits to Switzerland to bring back reports on German affairs for the Sûreté – and was later shot as a German spy. Almereyda began to live in style. His anarchist friends no longer visited him. Enemies talked of his houses, his cars and his girls . . . His health (never good) was failing and he took to morphia. Then in 1917, shortly after the French Mutinies, he was arrested. A few days afterwards he was found strangled in his cell, allegedly with a pair of bootlaces bought for him by his twelve-year-old son. An official statement said that he had died of a haemorrhage; a second statement said that he had committed suicide. It seems likely now that he was murdered – but by whose orders?

* P. E. Salès Gomès, *Jean Vigo* (Paris, Éditions du Seuil, 1957).

Jean Vigo always believed that Clemenceau was responsible. Others have argued that the murder was instigated by Malvy because Almereyda knew too much. Salès Gomès suggests a much simpler explanation: the police had a long standing feud with Almereyda which they had been unable to settle while he was protected by Malvy.

Vigo went to considerable lengths to clear his father's name; and he kept in touch with anarchist friends of the family, some of whom worked on his projects. At the end of his life, also, he was in two minds about joining the Communist Party. Still, how far do his films reflect or distort these political concerns? A Marxist critic, Bruno Voglino, claims that, 'Vigo unequivocally says "merde" to a world which he hated and which hated him'. Now Vigo did remember his father's sobriquet, and the excremental does play at least a nominal part in his work, as when the mutiny in *Zéro de Conduite* (the crisis of the film) is triggered off by one of the boys saying 'merde' to the headmaster. Nonetheless, his work is never sullen or rancorous – as Voglino appears to imply. Vigo doesn't give the impression of someone who hates the world, even the world of the bourgeoisie.

On the contrary, he is fascinated by the bourgeoisie, much as a child might be fascinated by a piece of broken glass. *À Propos de Nice* begins badly: aerial views of the town, palm trees, waves, skyscapes – amateur doodling; Vigo isn't engaged with his subject at this point. But the documentary does spring alive with a series of hand-held camera shots of the bourgeoisie as they take their Sunday morning stroll along the Promenade des Anglais: elderly pince-nezed gentlemen in gaiters, opulent ladies with boas. The camera lingers compulsively on clothes, legs and feet (especially feet). It is interesting to see, also, how these birds of paradise are related, by association, to the carnival and to its huge *papier maché* dummies with tiny grills in their necks – through which peer doleful operators.

The Promenade is continually returned to; and yet in this first sequence I must admit that Voglino is probably right.

Vigo goes in for some denigratory Montage à la Russe, inserting shots of alligators and giraffes; and at one moment the camera does swing away from the crowd to a roadsweeper shovelling up muck. Yet even here, I'm sure, Vigo isn't working purely for a satirical effect; to my mind we are back to the basic conflict in his style – between the squalid and the flamboyant, prison and fantasy. Presently this conflict deepens. People play at tennis and at bowls; yachts glide across the bay – all classes participate: and the camera and editing mime their harmonious movement. Then we are shown slum boys at play; but the camera dwells less on their games than on one boy's rickets and another's skin disease. It pans down to a shot of sewage in the gutters and to a cat, which might have belonged to Almereyda, eating refuse. At once Vigo cuts to a dance floor, then to a carnival and its Queen, a gentle *grande dame* in a coach, acknowledging roses offered to her by the crowd. At the close of this sequence we cut to Nice cemetery, and the camera moves slowly over discreet marble effigies.

Death and decay on one side, the finery and flamboyance of life on the other: we never seem to break away from this disturbing conflict. But by the final reel Vigo does point to a change – though this change is hardly less disquieting: factories belch smoke, create and purify their own waste. The carnival is over and the new age begins – but does Vigo really sympathize? The blazing furnaces look menacing; and we are far from reassured by glimpses of a grave-like hole and a mutilated carnival head, followed by a sustained shot of an elderly lady – member of the old regime – graciously chatting to someone unseen.

À Propos de Nice disturbs because one senses Vigo's own uncertainty. Personal problems war with political ones, and the personal ones win. What we *can* be sure about is Vigo's obsession. Still, what exactly is the source of his conflict? Most of the bourgeoisie shown are elderly and parental: could it be that Vigo is referring unconsciously to Almereyda, the anarchist who took 'merde' into his name and was seduced by the opulent life of the rich? In the cemetery scene, for instance, the camera dwells on the statue of a distinguished middle-aged man. Is Vigo paying respect to his father, as some critics assume; or is he merely poking fun at Mediterranean burial habits? Vigo himself was probably unsure.

In *Zéro de Conduite*, however, his anarchist sympathies do at first seem clear-cut. Here 'the hated world', the bourgeoisie, are represented by the school staff – a rum crew indeed. The headmaster is a shrill, bearded dwarf garbed in frock coat and bowler hat; the chemistry master is a randy, plump Captain Grimes; while the snooping supervisor Bec-de-Gaz is, as James Agee put it, like 'a tiptoeing lobster dressed in an undertaker's suit'. The one likeable master is Huguet, a new recruit, irresponsible and casual, a good mimic of Charlie the tramp. Vigo's notion of authority is plainly derisive – and at times this notion leads him to be crass. At one point the headmaster grows anxious because two of the boys develop an over-intense friendship and he warns the younger boy, the sensitive Tabard, of its dangers. Vigo sees the headmaster's concern as prurient; but how else does he expect the man to feel and act? Also Tabard, of all unlikely people, is responsible for starting off a mutiny. *Zéro de Conduite* was created out of the sensitive Vigo's own experience (*Ce film, c'est tellement ma vie de gosse que j'ai hâte de faire autre chose*), and he is still unable to detach himself from a boy's point of view. The fixation is understandable: Vigo had sore wounds; he knew what it was to be publicly 'exposed' – in his case as the son of an alleged traitor.

Does *Zéro de Conduite* display more than a schoolboy's contempt for authority – or rather, does the mutiny signify some wished-for social revolution? There is little evidence to support such a belief, even when we assume Vigo's necessary caution in stating it, or his technical difficulties in filming a mutiny – the narrative line becomes very scrappy in the final scenes. The masters are no more than Aunt Sallies, mere flies to wanton boys. We have no sense of an oppressive authority – the sort of thing likely to make one want to start lobbing bombs,

The school itself with its playground, fuggy classroom and bare kitchen is like a prison; but prisons are a *donnée* of the Vigo world, and no one would want to change that. Besides, as a symbol of revolution, the mutiny is very unusual. After Tabard had said 'merde' and triggered it off, we at once cut to the famous dormitory scene. Boys pillow-fight and drag about chamber pots; then, suddenly and oddly, the action goes into slow motion. Jaubert's music dissolves into an eerie, undefinable sound. The boys drift along the dormitory; some of them bear lanterns; before them rides their smirking leader carried on a chair. Goosefeathers fall like snow-flakes. The master's cubicle resembles a theatre, a shrine; and we are reminded of a carnival at Nice, of a religious procession, of fallen angels . . . The prison isn't destroyed but transformed by fantasy. Yet it remains a prison.

After this, the final sequence is, from the revolutionary point of view, something of an anti-climax: sport's day in the playground, where firemen perform gymnastics (with the neatness of Euclid) before a bevy of local dignitaries. No malice, no resentment – the glittering uniforms, all frills and curlicues, are splendid: the sequence has the delicacy of a René Clair comedy. The boys in full cry hurl stones at the firemen and the masters – who, implausibly pretending that the boys demonstrate for the visitors' benefit, rush their guests into the building and allow them to watch the shindig undisturbed. The boys climb on to the school roof and raise a pirates' flag.

In fact, to see Vigo's anarchism (or, if it comes to that, any form of anarchism) as revolutionary is to make nonsense of the film. Anarchists, I believe, are too angered by organization to be much concerned with worked-out programmes (as revolutionaries are); at best, they hope for some immediate release from tyranny. The mutiny in *Zéro de Conduite* allows the boys the pleasures of camaraderie and of a bust-up, but it offers no future; one cannot see the boys building their own ideal society.

Vigo doesn't blow up prisons in order to release their occupants: the explosion is pure fantasy and takes place in the mind. In this, one sees how his anarchism is closely linked to his use of surrealist techniques. 'The immediate reality of the surrealist revolution,' writes Sartre in *What is Literature?* 'is not to change anything whatever in the physical and apparent order of things as to criticize a movement in the mind'. Duchamp aims to destroy our assumptions about reality when he creates a lump of sugar in marble; we are shaken by its weight and its failure to melt. But in truth Duchamp doesn't destroy the object's essence, since this is impossible. What he does, instead, is to create an imaginary object. According to Sartre, surrealism liberates pure imagination and is 'the *only* poetic movement of the first half of the twentieth century'. Some of the surrealists, he believes, saw their movement as socially disruptive, but in this sense their achievement is almost wholly negative. Surrealism may weaken the structure of society by its undermining, say, of religious beliefs; it fails, however, to create a positive programme. 'We have no revelation, no intention of a new object, no seizure of matter or content – only the *purely formal* consciousness of the mind as a surpassing, an appeal, and an emptiness.' And Sartre, with the proud confidence of an engagé critic, quotes Hegel: surrealism 'penetrates this life like the spirit of a slave' – being an attempt to escape from consciousness of oneself and of one's situation in the world. It reflects rather than analyses the absurd and terrible experience of the First World War.

Vigo has had a noticeable influence on some of the New Wave directors; above all on Truffaut, who quotes heavily from *Zéro de Conduite* in *Les Quatre Cents Coups* (1959). But Vigo's influence is also more pervasive: a case could be made that from him, as much as from anyone else, stem the improvisation and technical freedom of the New Wave people – their use of slow motion, jump cuts and tracking shots. The director who uses this method of working may not be the final arbiter of reality as Buñuel is, say, in *Le Chien Andalou*, but he is at least its conscious master; we aren't allowed to forget his play of mind. Still, though Vigo isn't a radical in the Sartrean sense, we can hardly say that his work is no more than 'a *purely formal* consciousness of the mind – a surpassing, an appeal and an emptiness'. (A case one can sometimes make against the narcissism of Jean-Luc Godard.) The world may be a prison which Vigo transforms – blows up into glittering fragments or wrenches out of context; but at any rate we are not allowed to forget that first and foremost it *is* a prison.

It is likely, though, that Vigo found his obsession with prisons and fantasy too constricting; in his last film, anyhow, he managed partially to escape from it. But his last film also killed him. His health was never good, and the effort of making *L'Atalante* (1933–34) so lowered his resistance that it brought on a chronic attack of the pulmonary infection from which he died at the age of twenty-nine. (With the bitter knowledge of knowing that his distributors were mutilating the film to make it more commercial – the original copy was only more or less reconstituted after the Second World War.)

How did he manage to make this partial escape? In his autobiography, *Return to Yesterday*, Ford Madox Ford tells of an anarchist dinner at the old Holborn Restaurant, and of how some of the anarchists swore that the best way to achieve their aim was to throw bombs, and of how they were countered by Prince Kropotkin who said that love alone could establish the kingdom of God on earth. Two kinds of anarchism: and in *L'Atalante*, one of the most persuasive love stories in the cinema, Vigo changed sides to become, as it were, a disciple of Kropotkin. The story is of a country girl, Juliette, and her marriage to Jean, captain of a barge *L'Atalante*; and of how Juliette's loyalty to her husband is tested on three occasions. These temptations all take the form of fantasies, and so are similar to the bomb-throwing type of anarchism – as the first temptation makes clear. On the barge besides the two lovers is an old man, Père Jules (Michel Simon), and a boy (one of the

25

principal actors in *Zéro de Conduite*). Vigo makes it plain that these two have much in common. Père Jules is an amiable and gross old man, willing to please; still, in his childish way he is jealous – like the boy he has no adult relationship and feels excluded from the marriage – and his jealousy takes the form of complaining at the manner in which Juliette has disrupted routine on board (as though it hadn't been chaotic before). He doesn't realize that things are going badly with the two lovers. Juliette, now sexually awakened, is restless; her husband spends too many nights at the barge steering wheel. She becomes curious about Père Jules, and one day visits his cabin.

In this remarkable sequence Vigo gives us some idea of whom the old man is supposed to represent: for example, he is adept at using a sewing machine, a knack probably picked up in prison, and the cabin swarms with cats. Its constricted space, mingling filth and opulence, is packed with exotic debris, including a puppet orchestra conductor stolen from a carnival at Caracas, a music box, harpoons, a gramophone with a horn. Juliette is enchanted with these toys, but troubled when she finds in a cupboard a pair of hands pickled in a bottle of brine – all that remains of Père Jules' best friend. Jules can barely resist touching Juliette's hair, and seeks to entertain her by taking off his shirt to show her the marvels of his completely tattooed, obese belly.

In fact, Jules is hardly the kind of man to tempt Juliette into adultery; but the exoticism of this incident does warn us of a danger. Given the right conditions Juliette, like Madame Bovary, could be destroyed by her need for fantasy. Love integrates: but the things in the cabin are both a disorder and a disruption, wills o' the wisp of the mind; having the seductive power of a surrealist fetish (the idea of the severed hands is probably derived from *Le Chien Andalou*). Jean appears to realize this danger when he breaks in to the cabin to tell Jules that his rubbish stinks and should be thrown out. He may be jealous, in fact, but his denunciation and smashing of these things is understandable; they *are* potentially dangerous.

The second and more immediate threat to the marriage takes the guise of a hawker – an Ariel, as somebody has said, to Jules' Caliban. He is a young popinjay, in his slick way attractive; but, in spite of his smiles and wish to please, as lonely as Père Jules: in reality, a one-man band. He offers Juliette silks, perfumes, and trinkets more alluring than any of the debris in the cabin. He is a confidence trickster, if only because he plays on Juliette's confidence – and he soon ends up in a fight with Jean. But the hawker does mention another lure which is far more insidious than himself; and this, the promise of an enchanted city, is Paris itself. As he says,

'C'est un lot, c'est une affaire. Une ville qui pète feu. La ville lumière à tous les étages. En voulez vous des élégance? Des vitrines. Des vélos, des motos, des autos à capots pour Toto Parigot. C'est beau. Les Champs-Elysées pour Bébé, les Tuileries pour Bibi, Notre Dame pour Madame. C'est dit. Je vous enlève. Un fois, deux fois. Trois fois. Personne ne dit mot?'

This untranslatable Archie Rice type dialogue gives some idea of the vivacity of *L'Atalante*; but beneath its coruscation what precisely is the lurking danger? Later in the film Père Jules believes he is playing a gramophone record with his finger nail – in fact his boy assistant is playing a hand accordion at the same time – and defends his credulity by saying: 'You've seen far more extraordinary things than a disc that works by finger nail. Electricity, do you know what electricity is? Or the radio?' Vigo, I think, is showing us how surrealism is possibly the most fruitful way to express our sense of dismay and wonder in an age of scientific marvels – marvels that dupe the senses and may leave us a prey to superstition. As far as this goes, Vigo *is* a social critic and does refute Sartre.

Juliette's first awareness of Paris comes, significantly, when she first hears a radio – a bulletin announcing the spring sales. When the barge reaches Paris she tries to get her husband to

27

take her into the city, but by a mishap he is unable to do so. Against his wishes she goes alone – and he, in a moment of pique, sails the barge further up the river. But by another mishap Juliette is unable to follow him: her handbag is stolen by a starving pickpocket who is later seized, as in the best anarchist cartoons, by a brutish mob. She is in despair; she can't find work; the unemployed queue up outside the factory gates. At first Paris *did* offer her a dream – of fairy lights and, more ominously, of her shabbily dressed self, reflected in the glass of elegant shop windows. But quite literally she has missed the boat. Snow falls, and the streets are virtually empty; a man tries to pick her up. There is nothing sentimental about these scenes: Vigo is austere, uses long shot – he knows when *not* to quote from Chaplin. Exhausted, Juliette wanders to the city outskirts, to where the underside of civilization is exposed: twisted girders, discarded boilers, the Seine oily with sewage. The dream spirals down into a nightmare, from which she is only released when Père Jules finds her working in a gramophone shop and takes her back to the barge.

This story, claims Jean-Paul Marquet, ends on a note of despair – the lovers are condemned to a life of misery together. Again one disagrees: *L'Atalante*, though saturated in melancholy, is never pessimistic. It is witty – Vigo has an unceasing talent for creating gags; it is robust; and it celebrates a love affair which looks like developing after its early vicissitudes into a highly satisfactory marriage. Vigo himself was happily married and, I guess, must have felt his marriage to be his one protection against an often treacherous world. If anything, his argument in *L'Atalante* is that people can *only* be happy through a love based on trust.

On a realistic level, this relationship is drawn with great understanding. Above all, Juliette's feelings are magnificently evoked: her sense of being a chattel when she is first swung onto the barge like a bag of coals, and the vigour with which she takes over the domestic side of barge life by hauling a washtub onto the deck and ordering the three males to bring her their dirty linen (much to Père Jules' disapproval). The character of Jean is, perhaps, less successful. His anger on learning that Juliette has gone into Paris, and his spiteful decision to move the barge up the Seine seem too hysterical in light of the facts; he behaves as though Juliette had committed adultery. And his grief when he realizes his loss is also excessive. (Vigo was probably trying to play against the effect of Jean Dasté's somewhat phlegmatic style of acting).

These flaws are hardly noticeable, though, since the relationship's power over us doesn't depend on its realistic truth alone. The lovers are frequently shown, either together or separately, as lying on their bunks dreaming; and this idea gradually builds up into a cross-cutting sequence at the climax of the film when the two of them, miles apart, twist and turn in bed as though in telepathic communication. Dreams are part of the actual world, and, as Vigo realized, for lovers especially the two often mingle. By bringing such a resonance to the marriage he is able to make it appear as both subtle and rich. At times he shows its development in terms of a dreamlike losing and finding. Fog descends around the barge, and Jean, with a premonition of loss, goes on deck. He calls his wife's name, stumbles, then dimly sees her through the fog, a ghostly figure by the helm. In *L'Atalante* such sharp, incandescent moments recur again and again, and are often crystallized in one shot alone – much as were moments of fantasy in *Zéro de Conduite*. But *L'Atalante* is never surrealist; the dream tides, however bizarre, always flow beneath a realistic surface. Vigo's lyricism is remarkably concise: Juliette's loneliness and diffidence on the wedding night is evoked by *one* distant shot of the barge at dusk where, silhouetted by her white bridal dress, she waits for her husband on deck while around her the dark grey water moves swiftly. Or, again, passion is evoked in *one* image (reminiscent of Kokoschka's painting *Le Tourbillon des Vents*), when Jean lifts her into his arms and the breeze swirls her dress. We remember this image later as Jean, after losing his wife, plunges

into the river in the hope that the water will recall her to him.*
And she does appear: a swirling vision in white. Vigo's imagery
gives depth to a novelettish plot: the structure of *L'Atalante*
relies less on its narrative than on the association of these
images – 'a string of pearls' as one critic has said – capable of
an almost infinite extension; so that the film, even though
the extant copies are all mutilated, seems stylistically coherent.

This style has had a considerable influence on a number of
directors including, of all people, Fellini. The final scene in
I Vitelloni is similar to, and creates the same impression as the
scene after the wedding when the barge pulls out from the bank
and Juliette's relatives are shown as drifting away from us in a
series of tracking shots. But Fellini's imagism is much coarser –
is laid on with a thicker brush.

In Vigo's case, this style arises from a deeper concern, probably aroused by his awareness of what marriage meant to him:
that life involves processes (or rhythms) over which men have
little or no control. In *À Propos de Nice* we have an intimation
of such an interest, in the contrast between the vitality of the
carnival and its threat, the decay of the slums. In *Zéro de
Conduite* the boys' mutiny is like a disease that rises up and
destroys those who have neglected the source of infection,
much as in *Bleak House* poisoned air spreads from Tom-all-
Alone's. In *L'Atalante*, however, Vigo stresses mostly forces
of growth and health. The film opens with a wedding: an acceptance, if anything is, of the human condition – and this theme
is brought out movingly in a shot of the newly wedded couple
as they pick their way across a field, diminutive figures on the
horizon. The film also ends on this theme – a bird's eye view of
the barge as it steams up-river. And when chaos comes and
Jean loses his wife, his one hope is to refind these deep rhythms
of nature; suddenly and inexplicably he runs across the sands to
look out to sea (an idea echoed by Truffaut in the final moments

* An idea developed from his short film on a noted swimmer, Taris.

of *Les Quatre Cents Coups*). No doubt Vigo was stimulated by the Russian film-makers who have this visionary quality in abundance; but in his wry and delicate way, he makes it his own.

Robert Bresson

B

Prison cells and metaphors of incarceration – of the body, of addiction, even of the gross world itself – also haunt the imagination of Robert Bresson. Yet one scene alone, from *Un Condamné à Mort s'est Echappé* (1956) shows how far we have moved from the work of Jean Vigo. Fontaine, the protagonist, is just about to make his escape from Montluc prison when his plan is put in jeopardy; another prisoner, Jost, is ushered into his cell. Two worlds meet. Fontaine, man of honour, middle class aristocrat, all of whose efforts have been directed towards escape (not for him a Vigo-like acceptance of prison) looks suspiciously at the dishevelled, proletarian Jost – who might be straight out of *Zéro de Conduite*. Is Jost an informer, or can he be trusted? Fontaine *must* free himself (he is nothing but a will to freedom); and so, putting doubts aside, he decides Jost must come with him. The escape takes place and it succeeds. Only then do we realize that without Jost Fontaine, ironically, would probably have been unable to scale the final wall.

Dependence, then, is acknowledged. But this is no Vigoesque dependence, of men accepting their equality to one another. The relationship is more archaic, even feudal – reminiscent of Don Quixote and Sancho Panza, of Robinson Crusoe and Man Friday. As they reach freedom, Fontaine remains more or less in draughty self-possession. It is Jost who says (pure Vigo) that he wishes his mother could see him now.

Bresson was born in 1907. Since making his first feature *Les Anges du Péché* in 1943, he has made only five films – all of them exceptional, at least two of them masterpieces. But for the critic these films are delicate nets to untangle descriptively, if only because they soon snarl him up in paradox. In a sense, they are like those pellucid and reasonable arguments devised by theologians to help us transcend the faculty of reason.

Le Journal d'un Curé de Campagne (1950) opens on a country priest writing in an exercise book, 'I see nothing wrong in noting here, day by day, with complete frankness, the very humble and insignificant secrets of a life which is, however, without mystery.' This promise is kept; even so, the meaning of this life (and Bresson is Romantic enough to believe that a man's life of any worth is a continual allegory) can only be caught in the opaque final words, 'All is Grace.' Everything is shown, yet nothing is explained. Why must the country priest destroy himself in pursuit of a vocation beyond his physical resources? Why is he somehow set apart from other men? Questions like these are opened freely, like doors, only to be later slammed in our face.

The paradoxes of Catholic phenomenology – the hopeless effort to clarify the obscure workings of Grace – lead in turn to paradoxes of form. Film by film, Bresson has pared away irrelevancies in an attempt to show only the main stations in his heroes' progress towards Grace. But in so 'purifying' the world, he has only made it more constricted. The more clearly we see the way in which his heroes are liberated from the world/prison, the more firmly do they appear imprisoned in it – almost on the principle that a furnished room, with all its visual distractions, will seem far less of a prison than one that is bare and un-accommodating.

But there is another paradox of form which is just as intrinsic to his style, and which (for me at least) provides its teasing fascination. I think that Marianne Moore's definition of good poetry summarizes it best: 'imaginary gardens with real toads in them.' Bresson makes use of naturalistic motifs – motifs consisting of observable facts, especially of people in action – but he puts them together in what seems at first an arbitrary manner. All the same, in order to see *how* he puts these motifs together, we need to know exactly what they are.

The Real Toads. Bresson goes to considerable lengths to verify the empirical truth of his motifs. Behaviourism, you might argue, is the psychological counterpart of Naturalism (both doctrines stem from certain nineteenth century conceptions of science); and a behaviourist could hardly fault Bresson's picture of how people act. Fontaine's escape, and the almost dramatic role played by a spoon and a door, are filmed with the same care for detail that one would expect from a documentary about computers. It is as though human activity could be shown not in terms of motives, but of processes – of causes and effects, every one of which is demarcated. Bresson has long wanted to take this behaviourism to an extreme and to make a film limited entirely to a play of hands, glances and objects. It could be maintained, in fact, that at one point in *Pickpocket* (1959) this ambition does take over and distracts us from the theme of Michel's journey towards Grace. At this point the film turns into a lyrical documentary – though the lyricism is as detached as a time and motion study. For hours Michel practises his black art alone, as sternly as a virtuoso pianist. He slips watches off water pipes, slides wallets through newspapers and flexes his fingers. Things take on unusual qualities: a skirting board becomes the edge of a treasure chest, and wallets, watches and newspapers turn into magical properties like the toys of a conjurer. Then, when Michel meets his accomplices in a distant bar, this prestidigitation grows into a grand wallet of wallets gliding through jackets from pocket to hand against the sonorous chords of Lully's music. The ballet reaches its climax on a sunlit railway station at the seemingly dead hour when passengers wearily climb on to trains and prepare for the journey. With pickpockets around, this moment takes on a mysterious vitality as shifting wallets glitter, and hands like cobras rustle through pockets. In a sense, the bravura quality of this sequence provides its own undoing; it remains an anthology piece.

But Bresson seeks for real toads in other ways. For instance, he prefers amateur actors to professionals – on the rather questionable grounds that they are more authentic. Theoretically, he makes a good case for his choice. The professional, he believes, offers a too simplified image of human beings: he gives an *interpretation*; he takes us into the realms of artifice. 'Films, in which actors appear,' he says, 'are like those tormenting dreams in which we are forced against all reason to stick on to a face of someone familiar to us a nose or mouth which we know doesn't belong to them.' Bresson is no surrealist; he doesn't want to tamper with Nature, not at any rate *within* the motif. What he wants primarily from his actors is spontaneity. 'A genuine glance isn't something you can invent. When you catch it, it's admirable.' The professional actor is too defensive to be spontaneous; he is all technique and calculation. Yet Bresson is no De Sica when it comes to amateurs; he doesn't allow his actors to behave naturally. Needing a certain style, he forces them to restrict their facial expressions and to recite their lines so flatly that we might see them, not too fancifully, as automata. Real toads and imaginary gardens: in his search for a balance between spontaneity and formal convention, Bresson can sometimes tilt the scales towards the most false kind of artifice.

Yet the problem facing him isn't to be sniffed at. The true voice of feeling – a product of artifice – is hard to sustain at the best of times, and in an age when lyrics are more than usually fragmented, and in which the authentic is seldom more than briefly obtained, we should be grateful that even in *Pickpocket*, where Martin Lassalle as Michel is unable to pull together his part into a credible interpretation, there are moments when we can discover what Marianne Moore called 'a place for the genuine.'

Bresson takes great trouble in discovering these places, and even resorts – surprisingly, for so controlled a director – to improvisation. '*Je vais me faire des surprises*,' he says, quoting Valéry. 'It's not what actors show me that's important. It's what they hide . . .' And, of course, there is no toad more real than improvisation, which could be described as Naturalism's last stand to keep up appearances. Those incalculable moments placed within an ordered imaginary garden give us a sense of looseness within constriction; at times, of a newsreel edited into a sublime art.

Bresson thinks of himself not as a *metteur en scène* but as a *metteur en ordre*, as someone who puts together images much as an architect may create an inspired building out of dull bricks or concrete slabs. And, in fact, his images are never obtrusive; their power, rather, is generated by their relationship to one another. T. S. Eliot's definition of a good verbal style could apply to this film style – 'the common word exact without vulgarity, the formal word precise but not pedantic, the complete consort dancing together.' Bresson is always austere and straightforward; when possible he prefers the close-up, the most functional of camera movements, and a diffused greyish light. (His director of photography since *Le Journal* has been Léonce-Henri Burel.) You often need to see his work a second time to appreciate the art that goes into its beautiful sobriety.

It is made up, then, of elements of rapportage. Bresson, you could say, believes that the artist can record the truth directly, that appearances don't lie. He is at the antipodes to Ophuls and Welles (who claims to loathe his films), whose toads are as illusive as their gardens are imaginary. Unlike them, Bresson doesn't see the world as an ever-dissolving dream, a series of impressions as deceptive as the reflections in a witch's ball. In his gardens the real toads remain real, and their reality is unquestioned: the material world has a purpose, though its purpose may be obscure – has natural laws that can be discovered, though mankind may distort or misunderstand these laws.

Bresson wishes to give us the literal truth even at the cost of losing our sympathy. His *Procès de Jeanne D'Arc* (1962) appears cold, especially when compared to Carl Dreyer's *La Passion de Jeanne D'Arc* (1928). Based on the original transcript of the trial, it serenely presents us with the facts, and nothing but the facts. Dreyer's Joan is isolated; there is always the possibility that she might be wrong, and that God is not with her. Bresson's

Joan is already with the Saints, and her acute suffering is already seen as a cause for rejoicing.

In just the same way *Un Condamné* is more or less what its title claims it to be – the account of an actual escape. 'This story is true,' writes Bresson in the opening titles, 'I give it as it is, without embellishments.' Everything was done to fulfil this claim, and André Devigny who made the original escape was on hand throughout the filming to check every detail. Yet from its opening moments, even, we would be correct in guessing that *Un Condamné* is more than a documentary; for against the titles is played an extract from Mozart's Mass in C Minor – and from this precise choice of music we can justly infer that Bresson is expecting us (as Renoir sometimes does) to measure the present against the highest intellectual and moral standards of the eighteenth century. Besides, the Mozart is devotional music – and we should be warned that on one level at least the theme of liberation may be a metaphor for one man's progress towards God.

The Imaginary Gardens. At first we don't find it hard to orientate ourselves. Bresson is typical of many Romantics in his yearning for the neo-classical ideals of form and convention. The plot structure of a Racine tragedy is recreated in *Les Dames du Bois de Boulogne* (1945); its Cocteau script is in fact based on a story to be found in Diderot's *Jacques le Fataliste*, of a jealous woman, Hélène, and the revenge she takes on her ex-lover. Much of its fascination comes from the playing of eighteenth-century manners against a backdrop of motor-cars and nightclubs, and of making a convincing style out of this contrast.

Bresson is also neo-classical in his treatment of motifs. He keeps them to a minimum (which heightens the sense of austerity) and develops them through repetition and changing contrasts. M. Jean Sémolué has written vividly about the rondo form of *Le Journal*; but what strikes me most about its form is the *disjunction* of its motifs. 'A film,' says Bresson, 'should have the rhythm of writing, of a beating heart.' As far as I know,

40

the fade-out has never been used so positively, and with such effective and precise timing, like the closing of weary eyelids. Break a jar; then try to remake it out of fragments and a memory, and you will begin to understand its shape. To see a Bresson film is to undergo a lesson in form – in form as sensuously perceived. We are always aware of how the totality is made up out of well ordered fragments; and an art of fragments, as Bresson's films and the poetry of T. S. Eliot demonstrate, can often have the force of aphorism. Aphorisms are compact. They may give the impression of coldness, of keeping us at one remove; but because of this they can, too, be memorable and complete.

Outwardly Bresson's heroes are also neo-classical; they have all the trappings of their seventeenth-century prototypes – they tend, for instance, to have one passion or addiction which they act out uncompromisingly. Fontaine never questions his impulse to escape, never suffers doubt or apathy. His parents send him a parcel; it contains clothes (such as pyjamas and a scarf) which he at once tears up to make a rope. As in the case of Michel, the things about Fontaine are seen only as a means to an end. He is challenged to make the most from the least: the wire on his bed helps to bind the rope; his spoon makes a lever to open the cell door. Bresson is adept at showing how banal objects take on a fresh significance when put to an extraordinary use. When we are in a state of intense feeling, we think we perceive the physical world quite differently – the world is transformed. This transformation is all the more astonishing when it is conveyed detachedly to an audience (as in this film) through such limited means.

But unlike Racine's Phèdre, who lives on solid ground and whose passion can be understood as a disease blurring true perception, Bresson's heroes appear to act out their obsessions in a world without natural logic, in which their obsessions are the one certainty and so the only standard of judgement. The Naturalism of Bresson's motifs puts an irresistible pressure on us to expect the usual sorts of explanation for behaviour;

41

but Bresson often ignores motives, quite deliberately. We never learn why Fontaine is imprisoned, why the country priest is snubbed by his parishioners, why Michel is able to go abroad without a passport. These are only a few of the many motives withheld. Because of this unresolved pressure, his heroes arouse a considerable unease in me.

For a long time now Bresson has wanted to make a film based on Madame de Lafayette's *The Princess of Cleves*. The princess is an embodiment of virtue, and it is easy to see why he is interested in her. All his main characters are exemplary, and all of them (save for Hélène) are exemplary if not of goodness, at least of Grace. But such a meaning isn't woven into the fabric of some moral or natural order; rather, it is disconnected from the present world in which the action takes place, isolated, like a relic from some simpler, brighter, and more assured age, when such values were generally accepted. Bresson's art is seigneurial, created in a time when the social and moral orders on which it depends have crumbled away. It works in a void, and its ambitions must strike us, nowadays, as quixotic.

True, Bresson may convince us when he shows how eighteenth-century standards of integrity continue into the present. But doubts about the coherence of his world arise when he tries to give proof of how contemporary life reveals the (to me) petrified dogmas of Roman Catholicism. The effect is forced. The generalizations of theology don't emerge convincingly from the given facts. How can Bresson chart, say, the progress of a country priest towards Grace, while limiting the action to parish business? In part, certainly, through the contours of plot. Plot gives shape to the evidence and brings out the underlying theme. All the same, I suspect that someone who had never heard of the soul would probably find these plots very hard to understand; as it is, the references to Grace at the end of *Pickpocket* and *Le Journal* must come as a surprise to someone who isn't a Roman Catholic. Willing as I am to go along with the conventions of Bresson's imaginary garden, I still find it difficult – even after a number of viewings – to accept his interpretation of the country priest's life, and have to fight hard against the temptation to see the priest as a person with a strong instinct for self-destruction.

Bresson, I would suggest, hangs himself with his own behaviouristic rope. He forces us to realize that the gap between observed behaviour and Catholic theology is never resolved – that the real toads squat incongruously in these imaginary gardens. Of course, many of his paradoxes vanish once we make the often unconscious leap into thinking along his lines. The 'hey presto' of Grace, after all, does wonders in reconciling paradoxes. When they are blessed by it, people can be both free *and* predetermined, spontaneous *and* machine-like. 'Ah Jeanne, what a curious path I had to take,' murmurs Michel to his girl friend at the end of *Pickpocket*. The image of paths suggests tracks already worn and determined – and, in truth, these characters seem unable to escape their destinies. Their lives are measured out in a predictable cause and effect: Fontaine *must* liberate himself, Michel *must* pick pockets, the country priest *must* fulfil his vocation. At the same time, they have freedom of choice. A priest gives Fontaine the text, 'Marvel not I said unto thee, Ye must be born again. The wind bloweth where it listeth, and thou hearest the sound thereof, but canst not tell whence it cometh and whither it goeth.'

Fontaine's escape is a fluke. When a friend, Orsini, tries to break out of prison and is caught and shot, another prisoner tells Fontaine that Orsini had to fail so that he might succeed. But success is never certain. There is always a double focus: on action as seen with the hindsight of history, and on action *as lived now*. The hero may tread the well-worn path to Grace; but he is also enmeshed in the moment, the future uncertain and waiting to be created. The mood of these films is urgent. The hero is confronted by a series of important decisions, and he must choose. Intellectually, Bresson may be on the side of the angels and the supernatural, yet he is artist enough to value the importance of real toads and to know he must compromise.

He knows that in order to renounce the world he must first simulate its immediate demands.

This strategy requires the most uncommon tact, sometimes lacking; as in the final moments of *Le Journal* when the screen fades into an image of the Cross. On the other hand, the ending to *Procès de Jeanne D'Arc* is beautifully impersonal in its ambiguity. The authorities order that all of Joan's possessions should be burnt with her so that no possible relics might remain. But this order of theirs can be understood as a seal on Joan's triumph – that both she and her possessions are purged from the world. We are left with an image of a charred stake pointing up to the sky. From one viewpoint, the flames have destroyed Joan; from another, Joan has been purified.

Purification, indeed, is the key term in any discussion of Bresson's work. More than a theme, it describes his intentions: his wish for a 'pure' cinema uncontaminated by literary or theatrical effects. It describes his development also; the manner in which the fuss of plot gives way to a 'pure' event, such as a trial or an escape. A paring away of this kind has its value. Not least, it builds up concentration and contains our laughter. No one would dare be amused when Fontaine empties his slop bucket to the sound of a Mozart Mass.

In *Procès de Jeanne D'Arc* most of the action consists of a dialogue between Joan and her leading inquisitor – an antiphony of voices, interspersed by short scenes in Joan's cell. The static camera is held at middle distance. Shots are seldom varied, and contrast is provided by the abrupt fading out of sequences. Sound effects are limited and monotonous: feet scrape, quills scratch – any change in sound or image is startling. The device is brilliant. By isolating the effect of these trivia and by heightening them, Bresson makes us realize how important this trial is. We are at a watershed in history, and every act requires an intense scrutiny. Before our eyes history becomes eschatological.

But purity in art, as in sex, is often akin to frigidity. The country priest may renounce the world, but even at the moment when he realizes the cost of such a renunciation – as he rides on the pillion of his friend Olivier's motorcycle – his loss doesn't appear to be more than a token one. We never feel the agony endured by Jean-Pierre Melville's eponymous hero in *Léon Morin, prêtre* (1961) as he turns away from profane love. The Bresson hero is cold, and for him love, it appears, is hardly more than a gesture. (M. Sémolué finds it useful to compare Devigny's affection for Giminez with Bresson's transposition, Fontaine's mere civility towards Jost.) They are like high priests, these heroes, and it would be easy to see them as reflections of their creator who is, if anyone, the de Gaulle of the French cinema. Bresson's art is an attempt to preserve a tradition, to carry the doctrines of Roman Catholicism into the twentieth-century unadulterated. He observes the letter of the law; refuses amelioration or complicity. His heroes are set apart, and even the country priest is presented very much as one of a 'pure' race of aristocrats. Olivier tells him that he would make a good member of the Foreign Legion (to which Olivier belongs); and both the vicar of Torcy and the atheist doctor claim that he is of their heroic kind. As far as the action goes we seldom see him with the dross of common laity. His parochial life centres on the lord of the manor and his family. These aristocrats, as pure and hard as silver, have none of the obliging nobility of their counterparts in, say, Claude Autant-Lara's *Douce* (1943). They are as uncompromising as the priest, and the ironies arising out of their conflict are bitter and needless.

The novels of Montherlant and Evelyn Waugh give ample proof of how people who think of themselves as a race apart prefer to believe themselves rejected if they cannot sustain the pretence of being thought superior. And sometimes the country priest behaves as though he too were a *maudit*; as when, on virtually no evidence, he believes he is ignored or reviled by his parishioners. If there was less of a disparity between the casting of the delicate actor, Claude Laydu, and the character of the priest, we would see how he is much closer to the peevish Hélène than Bresson would probably want to admit to.

Bresson may be an eccentric in the cinema of today, but this doesn't mean that he should be peripheral to our attention. Nowadays, when experience appears to have no centrality, many serious artists are forced by their investigations into some kind of eccentricity. In finding areas of his experience meaningful, the artist is yet unable to relate these areas to any general framework of ideas and is often driven into creating his own homespun philosophy.

Some directors behave as though they were resigned to this failure. Godard, who acknowledges a debt to Bresson, puts together his often improvised fragments in a self-negating manner, as if he knew that any attempt at commitment were bound to fail. Biting insights are unrelated to any kind of positive world view; hence the uneven quality of his work, as careless as the doodles of a genius. At most, we can say that he is, perhaps unconsciously, an adherent to the one ideology that proclaims such a failure – existentialism.* Drawn back on to his own resources, Godard's one commitment and principal theme appears to be the act of making films, the sheer joy of technical accomplishment. Other directors have done their best to integrate ideology and insight but seldom plausibly. Antonioni, for one, believes that his films explore the Marxist concept of alienation; and yet, as many critics have pointed out, there is a split between the richness of his *mise en scène* and the relative poverty of his argument. Alienation is merely an inadequate guiding line; the real content is more to be found in his visual appreciation of the world. What is the point of those choreographic camera movements in *L'Avventura*? Presumably they have a point, though I am not sure I know what it is. But these movements are too right aesthetically to be without some sort of conceptual meaning.

Bresson is a Romantic conservative yearning for a neo-

* Gabriel Pearson and Eric Rhode, *Cinema of Appearance*, Sight and Sound, Autumn 1961.

classical order, an idealized stability, which for him takes a Christian form: the Kingdom of God. Like Antonioni, he fails to discover received truths in the world. But the almost scientific caution with which he peers at human behaviour and notes all the evidence is undermined by his reckless *salto mortale* into the arguments of faith. Even so, technically, Bresson remains a pioneer. A conservative in political and social attitudes, he is still a radical when it comes to art. He is as much of the avant-garde as Robbe-Grillet, say, or Beckett. His method is similar to theirs – real toads in imaginary gardens – though he may appear less obscure than them, since we know more about the logic of his gardens.

Besides, though his lucid enigmas may be coldly aloof, they are also deeply moving – and moving in much the same way as the family sagas of Yasujiro Ozu. They recall those epic emotions engendered by resistance, loyalty, and meaningful sacrifice – those irrepressible 'psychic processes', which we might be tempted to dismiss carelessly (and falsely) as mere shadows of some ancient and long dead morality, all that is most obdurate in the conserving spirit of mankind.

Sergei Eisenstein

> 'Remember that your work will be judged by millions of people.
> You shouldn't invent images and events while sitting in your office.
> You must take them from life – learn from life. Let life teach you!'
>
> J. V. STALIN

The flag is neutral. The flag is a cypher meaning anything or nothing. It flies everywhere in this friendly bucolic town of Gothic rooftops and quaint chimneys. Wherever we turn we see this flag, if only out of the corner of our eyes. It swirls above water near a mill wheel, or by some children playing games, or peasants dancing in folk costume, or at a midnight sing-song lit by bonfires. The flag is always there. And gradually the flag begins to accrete meanings – of friendliness, warmth and protection. *And yet we are being tricked*, since in fact the flag remains neutral. The flag is a cypher meaning anything or nothing.

But the flag is only a harbinger of things to come. Soon it moves into the periphery of our vision as the crowds part and we see for the first time the Führer's face. Unlike the crowd, who must view him from afar, we have a privileged position. We see him in close-up. We see him during those nervous, almost droll moments before he enters the arena. We see him accept flowers from a little girl and talk to her as though he were her father. But when this thought of a father occurs to us we dismiss it with a smile; for we recognize that this figure before us, so diffident and detached from the pageantry of power, has nothing of the paternal about him. He is more like an elder brother about to restore the fortunes of a ruined

51

family. And we may be so pleased and moved by this thought that we fail to notice that Hitler's face is as blank as a flag. An occasional twitch of the cheek perhaps, an occasional gleam in the eyes – otherwise this face betrays nothing. It is a face that takes on meanings from our reading of the situation about it.

The craft of propaganda is nowhere more tested than when it becomes a trick to sell us short. Leni Riefenstahl's *Triumph of the Will* (1934) is a confidence trick of this kind – a quite conscious attempt to deceive us. For instance, what sort of film is it? We might be tempted to call it a documentary, the record of an actual event. But beware: the question is loaded, the trap prepared, the sleight of hand already begun. In fact, the movements at the Nuremberg Rally were mostly arranged so that the film could be made. The most casual effect is de- liberately planned; the crowds are drilled like film extras in an epic, and the twenty-three cameramen are everywhere. *Triumph of the Will* is a case, not of history being rewritten, but of history being faked as it takes place. In its disdain for all truth, it is a premonition of a nihilistic future. The beautifully modu- lated camerawork and the pageantry are as empty as writing on the air. And at the heart of it is the void of the flag and the face.

The main problem in creating propaganda is to find emblems that represent your viewpoint ('the good') and those of your enemies ('the bad'). Now it happens that *Triumph of the Will* isn't able to draw rhetorical strength from the same source as *Mein Kampf* – as an attack on the enemy. Its purpose is to make converts to Nazism and to influence people, and it does this (at least in its opening sequences) by playing on the isolation of the filmgoer and by arousing his need for companionship. Even so, in spite of her infatuation for Hitler, Leni Riefenstahl must have known she didn't have much of a case for this newcomer to the world scene. After all, he was hardly the stuff from which a Valentino is made, and his doctrines could hardly be offered up directly as sanctions of goodness. And so Riefenstahl doesn't choose blank emblems so much out of honesty (I assume) as out of desperate expediency. She was unable to suggest a positive in any other way.

But this device, however brilliant, was not discovered by her. In 1929, in a lecture to the London Film Club (later published in his *Film Technique*), V. I. Pudvokin had said, 'In the film of *The Heir to Genghis Khan* (*Storm over Asia*) I wanted to have a crowd of Mongols looking with rapture on a precious fox-fur. I engaged a Chinese conjurer and photographed the faces of the Mongols watching him. When I joined this piece to the shot of fur held in the hands of the seller, I got the result I required.'*

What Pudovkin is describing, rather crudely, is the principle of montage – the building up of a complex image out of pieces of neutral film. A colleague of Pudovkin's, Lev Kuleshov, who claimed to be its inventor, had described a number of experiments in the magazine *Kino-Phot* (No. 3), which illustrated the scope of this kind of editing. In one experiment the White House was made to appear in the centre of Moscow; in another, 'solely by means of montage we showed a living girl, but one who didn't actually exist, because we had filmed the lips of one woman, the legs of another, the back of a third, the eyes of a fourth.'

Of course, film-makers had long before discovered most of the possibilities of editing. Griffith's *Intolerance*, for instance, with its audacious cross-cutting between four stories had already been shown in the Soviet Union. What was new, however, was the breaking down of objects into parts so that they could be reconstructed as *original forms*. Montage works on the principle that two and two make five, or that the whole is greater than the sum of the parts.

It would be hard to underestimate the value of montage as an *idea* in the history of art, in its relation to Cubism, modernist

* I am indebted to Jay Leyda's *Kino* (Allen & Unwin 1960) for a number of the historical facts in this chapter.

poetry or some types of constructional sculpture. Significantly Eisenstein, like Pound and Apollinaire, was stimulated by the Japanese ideogram – 'one idea set up on top of another' (Pound) – and saw it as a form of montage. In the history of the cinema, though, montage has hardly proved seminal and the tradition appears to have foundered with the death of Eisenstein. Why so? To some extent, possibly, because montage breaks narrative flow; its construction of original entities tends to be cumbersome, and unlike pieces of sculpture creates entities that cannot be taken in at a glance.

At his best, Eisenstein could make a really profound use of montage. He had a sculptor's feeling for objects. They stirred his imagination, and informed his shaping of episodes. It was the sight of the marble steps at Odessa, for example, and the movement they suggested, that gave him the basic theme of *Battleship Potemkin* (1925). It seems he needed an object – a side of rotting meat or a piece of tarpaulin – as a turning point for each episode. But he couldn't leave these things alone. He had to take them apart and explore their properties. Leonardo da Vinci fascinated him as both artist and scientist; and it may be assumed (wrongly) that his own breaking down of things was similar to a scientist's exploration of reality, But how far was he able to put this misunderstanding to good account?

October (1928) opens with a shot of the Tsar's statue, and is followed by a series of shots framed on the various symbols of power – the sceptre, the crown, and so on – as they tumble off the figure, until there is nothing left on the pedestal. Eisenstein then reverses these shots so that the statue is reintegrated. Now this piece of montage is a neat way of showing the hollowness of authority. But as a stylistic device it also prepares us for later sequences, such as the one in which the city authorities order the bridges to be raised. Across the centre of one of these bridges lies a dead horse, attached to a carriage, and the corpse of a girl. As the bridge pulls apart the girl's hair slides sensuously across the widening gap, and the horse, held back by the

carriage from falling into the river, dangles over the edge –
until the bridge reaches such a height that the harness snaps and
the horse drops, like a dainty morsel into a spaniel's mouth.
What is so effective about this sequence is not so much the
bizarre location of the girl and the horse as the steady opening
of the bridge and the slow, vertical movement of its girders
which, like Fritz Lang's man-eating Moloch, cannot be resisted.
(This device is beautifully repeated much later when the girders
on another bridge are seen to move horizontally.) In fact this
idea – the breaking apart of things – recurs throughout the film,
and is taken to an extreme at the climax – the storming of the
Winter Palace. The mob burst through the gates and rush down
corridors, smash up wine cellars and loot drawing rooms.
This orgy is consummated when a soldier bayonets open the
mattress on the Tsarina's bed.

But the violence of this destruction, and the sheer pleasure
with which Eisenstein lingers over it, raises doubts about his
style. How far was he conscious of his ideas as coming together
in a pattern, or how far was he in the grip of some destructive
impulse that merely has an obsessional order? It is hard to say
– if only because Eisenstein can sometimes use montage con-
structively to build up three-dimensional objects. In *Ivan the
Terrible* (1945) the scowling Tsar, posing in his extravagant
robes, is made into more than a tailor's dummy by a great
number of static shots taken from many angles. A cup of poison
is also made substantial by just this sort of insistence. I am
reminded of how, during the war, a map of enemy terrain could
be built up by the putting together of numerous aerial photographs.

Even so, montage is always a risky technique, since it gives
the artist too much freedom. It all too easily becomes sub-
servient to the fantasies of its master, the creator and destroyer
of chimera – and if its master is as unsure of himself as Eisenstein presumably was when he filmed the Winter Palace sequence,
it can do him a great disservice. It is far from encouraging to
learn, for instance, that Eisenstein believed that montage should

affect an audience like a punch in the face. In 1929 he said,
'Content, as I see it, is a series of connected shocks and their
arrangement in such a way that they produce the desired reaction in correct proportion.' The psychology behind this statement is hopefully Pavlovian – but no more than hopefully so.
The method is too woolly to impress us as scientific. All too
easily Eisenstein's attempts to fragment reality could turn into
a contempt for objects and could strengthen his taste for a wild
and baseless rhetoric.

It is generally true that if a director takes up an authoritarian
position his style will be formalist and will approach the ceremonies of religion. In an essay on the Marxist painter Robert
Lapoujade, Jean-Paul Sartre has written, 'Good sentiments
tend towards formalism. If a feeling of righteous indignation is
to be communicated, the public must be able to decipher the
message; the anxieties of art must be subordinated to false
securities. The artist adopts the most legible transcription, which
is necessarily a conventionalized style.' Another explanation
would be to say that the more extreme the political stance the
more difficult it becomes to justify, since commonsense will
continually challenge its assumptions. And so the authoritarian
is liable to retreat into artifice, into the trickery of masks or the
violent and deceptive hues of melodrama.

At this point we see how much Riefenstahl and Eisenstein
have in common. Neither of them is interested in evidence;
both of them are concerned with the art of persuasion, with
using an elaborate technique to distract us while the propaganda goes about its business. But whereas the rhythms of
Riefenstahl's editing and camerawork induce in us a state of
semi-hypnotic acquiescence. Eisenstein's montage tends to pull
us up short, to make us admire his cleverness.

Their craft, indeed, is dazzling. It also illustrates the limitations of propaganda as a mode of describing the complexity of
human beings. However, Riefenstahl and Eisenstein appear
unaware of this limitation. They both trade happily in emblems

as though emblems were sufficient. Eisenstein may not have used flags and blank faces, but he does use something similar – the 'type' face. He had a wonderful talent for discovering 'type' faces, expressive of some class or profession; like Leonardo, he had a special feeling for the grotesque. Still, the complaint that his talent is best seen in still photographs, and so isn't primarily cinematic, has some justification. Frequently these 'type' faces are fixed in a scowl or a grimace, their fixity emphasized by static set-ups.

Not surprisingly, Eisenstein was able to use masks brilliantly, nowhere more so than in the 'Calavera' death day pageant of *Que Viva Mexico* (1931), where people wear skull masks and models of the skull can be seen everywhere. One by one people take off these masks to show smiling faces beneath, but beneath the final one (at least in Marie Seton's version of this unfinished film) there is a real skull. For once the significance of emblems is explored, in this case to make the point that death will eventually triumph over every defence, even contempt of death.

But then *Que Viva Mexico* is an unusual film in more than one way. It is the one occasion when, presumably under the influence of Mexico and the sun, Eisenstein moved away from the world of frozen gestures towards spontaneity and warmth. Here are faces that contain the mystery and tenderness of a Leonardo portrait – girls, like the appropriately named Concepçion, naked and with full breasts, basking in hammocks in stippled sunshine. There is no shame or prurience in these scenes. They are drugged with the unfulfilled sensual yearning that saturates this film, and which breaks through to us, like an ache, in the lingering shots of great echoing spaces, and of temples and ruins as habitual to this soil as some ancient forest. To Eisenstein Mexico offered release. No wonder he felt in the grip of such a compulsion that he went on filming long after his budget had run out.

It was one of the few occasions when he showed humility before the greatness of his subject. Admittedly, he was living at a time when humility was not held in much respect. The USSR was on the defensive, under threat from enemies both real and imagined; and the young Eisenstein was touchingly eager to promote the cause of the Revolution. But such a zeal was unlikely to lead to the disinterested pursuit of the truth. Moreover, he had been trained at the Proletkult theatre (insofar as he had any training), and the theatre of that time – very much under the influence of Meyerhold – enjoyed butchering texts in the name of experiment, so as to give a field day to the producer. Eisenstein was as clever at these games as anyone and could happily hire an acrobat or two to cavort through his production of Ostrovsky's *Much Simplicity in Every Wise Man*, or generally turn everything upside down.

So his art became one of manipulation and trickery, where individuals became emblems and groups of people became crowds, as smartly drilled as any opera chorus. But he ran into the same trouble as Riefenstahl. Reality proved obdurate. The emblems often failed to stick or seem appropriate. This is hardly unexpected, since emblems are usually difficult to manipulate. I can think of only one film where they are used with precision, Francesco Rosi's *Salvatore Giuliano* (1962). Rosi, also a Marxist, chooses the least troublesome of emblems to represent his hero – a corpse. In fact, *Salvatore Giuliano* is a tragedy about a community and not about an individual; the bandit's native village is firmly placed at the centre of the Action. Emblems are appropriate in this case because we are immersed in a society where hierarchy is everything, and everything lies in show. Motives seldom need to be given.

Rosi never cheats, never distorts history. But then he has no reason to, for history is on his side. Even now the Giuliano case is wide open; no one has worked out who was responsible for the intrigue surrounding the bandit's death. And so, though we have puppets in the shape of bandits, the Mafia, caribinieri, and officials, we never learn who pulls the strings. Rosi makes a style out of mystery; he ignores the causes of actions and concerns himself with their effect. When Salvatore's lieutenant is poisoned we neither see nor learn of the person responsible for his death. We are forced to concentrate on the imagery of the body writhing in a blanket. *Salvatore Giuliano* is made up of such baroque set-pieces as this. They are held up to the eye coldly and are usually filmed from a distance: the communists are massacred and their pennons flutter in the breeze; Salvatore's mother caws over her son's corpse like a crow. This is alienation to a purpose. We are never allowed to sympathize with these happenings; at the most we are excited by a display of energy. 'Impersonal energy', I would say, is the governing characteristic of this film.

But Eisenstein doesn't share Rosi's prudence in choice of subject, or his care (possibly encouraged by a fear for the laws of libel) in measuring out praise and blame. True, he has a flair for invective as in the case of *October*, where the idea of God is reduced to a series of images, descending from the most sophisticated of icons to the most primitive of carvings. And for some of the time his vignettes of millionaires and White Army generals are amusing; they make plausible monsters of fiction, and have enough coarse vitality to stop us questioning their truth in reality. But after a while the malice grows tiresome. Eisenstein overdoes his case, though his case may be a good one. His denigration of Kerensky – in his crosscutting to a peacock, or sneering parallels to Napoleon, or repeated clip of Kerensky walking up the same flight of stairs – is excessive and liable to win sympathy for the victim. It doesn't take us long to realize that Eisenstein, rather likably, is too lacking in guile to show much talent for propaganda.

As with Riefenstahl, he finds it hard to create emblems that stand for 'the good'. The screaming pretentions of such titles as 'All as before – /Hunger and War/ BUT/ At the Finland Station/ HIM!' are hardly justified by the romantic poster shot of Lenin gesticulating with an unfurled banner beside him. And we don't need to have seen the emblem he offers as his most substantial positive, his emblem for all that is best in the

Revolution – those beefy, scowling young members of the proletariat with their well-developed torsos – to guess that Eisenstein's fumbling, his inability to persuade us, is brought on by the pressure of a fantasy (or complex of fantasies) which is at odds with his intended theme.

'Without Leonardo, Marx, Lenin, Freud and the cinema,' he once said, 'I would possibly have been another Oscar Wilde.' This confession is painful. Eisenstein doesn't appear aware of how much he is revealing. He could be terribly vulnerable, at the mercy of inner threats: it is, for instance, his unquestioning submission to the cruel menace of his proletarian heroes, rather than his fascination with their torsos, which is disturbing. Even so, to say that he was vulnerable doesn't imply that he was open to experience.

Marie Seton's biography of him is far more valuable than her detractors allow. Still, I am far from convinced by the picture she draws of the sensitive artist gnawed by neuroses and forced, through shyness, to masquerade in public as a clown. In spite of his ebullience and great appetite for learning (ranging from Leonardo etc., to the cinema) Eisenstein had a remarkably *arid* mind – a mind ground small and dry by dogma. And his sensitivity, even towards the arts, was often blunted to the point of being obtuse. At times he could have done with some of the generosity of that figure he so greatly felt contempt for, Oscar Wilde.

Typically, and almost wilfully, he doesn't give us the humane and totally persuasive motives for the Revolution, such as we see in the Thorndikes' compilation, *The Russian Miracle* (1963): how in pre-Revolutionary Russia the workers were so exploited that at the Baku oilfields men were worn out and old by the age of thirty-five; how the slightest protest at the regime could be rewarded by the hundred days' (and often fatal) march to Siberia, followed by a long and dreadful period in the settlements there. None of this concerns Eisenstein. For him the Revolution is an exercise in revenge. The climax of *October* is given over to the sacking of the Winter Palace, and in no way illuminates the historical significance of the famous ten days. Actually, the importance this event took on in Eisenstein's mind (with the destruction of the Tsarina's bed as its centre-piece) is incommensurate with the facts of the case, and is as inexact as it would be to suggest that the French Revolution culminated in the storming of the Bastille.

Eisenstein had a remarkable talent for transmitting his fantasies on to the screen in such a manner that even now the concluding sequence to *Strike* (1924), in which the massacre of the workers is crosscut to an ox having its throat cut in a slaughter house, has the desired effect of shocking us. But the effect is little more than one of shock. Eisenstein made intellectual claims for montage and wrote of its dialectical nature; but as this typical example shows, these claims are hardly justified. These two images – of the dying workers and the ox – just don't synthesize into a complex new entity; nor does the cutting of the ox's throat deepen our understanding of the massacre.

And yet Eisenstein, I believe, was more confused than dishonest and didn't try consciously to trick his audience into an illusion of knowledge. A good case of such confusion is the murder of the student in *October*, after the failure of the uprising. A number of society women have this student at their mercy and attack him furiously with their parasols. The filming tempts us to sympathize with the victim. The elegant women in their white summer frocks look as monstrous as any of the gorgons in the plays of Tennessee Williams. But after the murder we are given a shot of the student's body as it lies on the waterfront, the neck lacerated by ferrules, the torso exposed. Our identification has shifted, it appears, from victim to oppressor. The layout of this composition leads us to think that it must have some special erotic significance for its creator, as though the student had become a St Sebastian.

When all is said and done, when we have acknowledged Eisenstein's often resourceful use of the medium and the latent energy of his ideas, we are still left in doubt about the value of his art – an art so self-destructive, so deracinated, so remote from the forces of growth. But to ask this question is to find oneself questioning a great deal of contemporary art. (And Eisenstein is important not least because he is so representative of this art.) The painter Francis Bacon, who admires him, is a case in point. Yet there is an ambiguity of form and texture in the best of Bacon's paintings which haunts us long after their initial impact. This ambiguity is seldom found in Eisenstein, and his imaginings soon grow oppressive. I can understand (without sympathizing) why the Soviet authorities thought of *October* as an unhealthy failure of the experimental cinema and thereafter griped and carped at all his work.

But on one occasion at least Eisenstein *was* able to use destructive fantasies in an enlarging manner – in the well-known Odessa steps sequence of *Battleship Potemkin*. Although this sequence does have quirky touches that betray personal animosities – why, for instance, does Eisenstein single out mainly bourgeois targets in the crowd, such as the woman with pince-nez, when his aim is to win sympathy for the oppressed workers? – the total effect has a generalizing power similar to Leonardo's *Notes on the Representation of The Deluge in Painting,* which Eisenstein referred to admiringly in his lectures. The catastrophe is made to appear so inevitable that it resembles a force of nature. Our feeling for the progressive descent of the steps is heightened by a slow and descending camera track shot; we have a sense of an irresistible crushing power. This effect is reinforced by shots framed on objects and parts of the body: the menacing statue that foreshadows the arrival of the troops; or the troops themselves seen in terms of raised rifles and jackboots marching down the steps; or the perambulator, gradually gaining momentum as it goes out of control; or the smashed pince-nez that recalls the doctor, who had been 'blind' to the maggots on the rotting meat, and whose pince-nez was found dangling on a length of rope after the mutiny. The world is fragmented. Human beings are dehumanized, are reduced to their attributes or possessions (even their shrieks and cries are necessarily silent), are no more than grist to this terrible machine of raised rifles and trampling jackboots. At best, they are 'types', such as the mother who moves defiantly up the steps and towards the troops, holding up her baby to them as a token of pity (much as a priest may hold up wafers before the altar to have them blessed), and yet who is shot down with everyone else.

This sequence is marvellous, and nothing else in Eisenstein's *oeuvre* makes me so regret the circumstances that crippled his talent. He was never again to use his fantasies in such a way as to give us a convincing picture of the world. In his later films, in *Alexander Nevsky* (1938) and the two completed parts of *Ivan the Terrible*, he abandoned himself to the self-indulgence of fantasy. He lowered his standards, and so was able to achieve a limited sort of perfection, These apparently historical sagas are glorified, superb boys' own stories – a pageant for paranoids, intrigue exercised for its own sake. In them Eisenstein exhibits a flair for decoration and for the heightened theatrical effect that has only been equalled since by the films of Cocteau and Visconti. But he never lets go, is always in control. The style is operatic, formalist, supremely authoritarian. Nicolai Cherkassov, who played Ivan, made a revealing comment, I think, when he complained that Eisenstein gave him no chance to act; he was continually made to pose, to contort into icon shapes. *Alexander Nevsky* and *Ivan the Terrible* are rigid in structure and ingrowing, so that menace breeds upon itself like a public disgrace.

An undercurrent of menace, indeed, always runs through Eisenstein's work, ill-defined, swirling about itself, surfacing most noticeably in the earlier films; it is there in the recurring image of guns pointing across a river before the view of a city, in those sullen youths, and, most poignantly, in the image from *Strike* of the small boy, oblivious of danger, wandering about between the horses' legs of the police cavalry, massing before a charge. Eisenstein was like this child, always trapped in a threatening situation and unable to find his way out – always trapped, maybe, because he never found a way (as Humphrey Jennings did) to align himself with some authentic positive, to some form of sustaining goodness.

Humphrey Jennings

c

> 'And the privy admonishers of men
> Call for fires in the City,
> For heaps of smoking ruins
> In the night of prosperity & wantonness'
>
> BLAKE – *The Song of Los*

Humphrey Jennings worked best when the things he loved were most under threat. He needed threat to shake him out of his natural reserve and bias towards pedantry – to force him into making films in a way which, earlier, he might have found tactless. He was an intellectual – yet threat revealed in him a lyricist, someone willing to celebrate the things he loved, and to expose the depths of his attachments.

The possibility of a German invasion gave one form to threat. There is a resilience, an urgency, an opening up of talent in *The First Days* (1939) and *Listen to Britain* (1941) which the pre-war films had given little promise of. *The First Days* provides a thumb-nail sketch of the phoney war. It opens on an English Sunday in London, peaceful and Georgian in mood: churchgoers, museums, soft clouds in the sky. But ease gives way to disorder; London prepares for the coming siege. 'Everybody,' says the over-idealistic commentary, 'was working for the public good.' People leave their damp basements or luxury flats to build earthworks and to fill sandbags. Children are evacuated; the city is drained of vitality. 'Funny,' says a housewife, 'needs a war to give us a bit of peace and quiet.' But the peace and quiet is menacing. The war, we are assured, is in the capable hands of the young. The older generation just need to

67

have patience, just need to wait. Meanwhile, the city is transformed: shop windows are boarded up, and gas masks and luminous paint appear everywhere.

Jennings was one of the organizers of the 1936 London Surrealist Exhibition; and his own paintings, I'm told, show the influence of Surrealism. Not so his films. At the most, Surrealism helped him to observe more closely, and to notice the incongruities of London under siege. 'It was he,' said John Grierson, 'who discovered the Louis Quinze properties in a Lyons' Swiss Roll.' A Christmas Island statue waits like a pudding beside the pseudo-Grecian pillars of the British Museum. The frames in the National Gallery are empty. The police are dressed like civilians, while most passers-by are in uniform. In *London Can Take It* (1940) people go to work in the City in a horse and cart; a woman enters a shop by its smashed window and buys a coat on display. But Jennings doesn't allow himself the wit of, say, a Magritte. At any moment now the invaders may land, and he, too, feels the gnawing ache of uncertainty (hard to imagine with the hindsight of twenty-five years). So Jennings is sober, cautious, delicate – nowhere more so than in the sequence where the soldier leaves his girl. None of the heroics or tears of *In Which We Serve*. Outside the station they pass a flower-seller, then say goodbye as the train leaves. The girl repasses the barrow and says 'no' to a proffered rose. 'People joked but in their hearts was devastation' – Jennings risks the ornate phrase, but his filming remains controlled. The final moments are taut with expectancy: soldiers in battle uniform guard the Palace gates, a barrage balloon floats above the Thames.

Listen to Britain is more openly Romantic in style. The threat is sharper – yet nothing happens. We are at once keyed up. The opening shots are of clouds, cornfields, a harvester; then a formation of Spitfires drones across the sky unendingly, and the corn sways. Dusk, and we are outside an isolated house, a dim lamp in one window. Sounds of a radio drift out to us – the six o'clock pips, and the beginning of the news. Jennings is adept at using the radio to raise tension. In an unseen war people just wait for the next bulletin – have they landed yet? what's going on in London?

Tension is also built up by contrast. Jennings cuts from the sea at twilight, sluggishly licking the shore, to the false gaiety of a dance hall – which he then abruptly undermines by further glimpses of the promenade; 'Roll Out the Barrel' barely heard in the distance, air-raid wardens silhouetted against a sombre seascape. The dancers, placed next to these suggested feints of war out at sea, look like nervous puppets – and, in retrospect, their dancing seems desperate. Jennings continues to repeat this image pattern: a night train grinds to a halt by a signal box, and within one of the brightly lit carriages Canadian soldiers sing a ballad to the sound of an accordion; then the dark engine steams into motion again. Night and day; stark collieries against glaring streets – Jennings arranges his material with a deft sense of rhythm. He has a musician's ear; indeed, the shape of his repetitions often suggests sonata form. Yet I never feel he imposes this form. The complex soundtrack (no commentary) is one of the most subtle in the history of the cinema.

Once or twice the *ideas* behind the editing seem crude (though the execution of them may be superb), as when Jennings cuts from a factory workers' playtime – Flanagan and Allen, cod and chips – to a Myra Hess concert at the National Gallery: but I suppose that Jennings had to use Mozart and the presence of Royalty to build up to the bravura of his closing moments. The Mozart piano concerto gives way to the thunder of a tank factory, to an impudent brass band, to welders hammering out blocks of steel (Los?), and then back to the cornfields and to a choir singing *Rule Britannia*. This brazen final touch is consummate and completely justified. At once the tight-lipped urgency, the great rhythms of *Listen to Britain*, take on full significance.

We never see the enemy; the threat remains implied. I find it

69

instructive to compare his underrated *The Silent Village* (1943) – which retells the story of the destruction of Lidice, but set in a Welsh hamlet – with *It Happened Here* (1964), directed by Kevin Brownlow and Andrew Mollo. Both films are about the possible Nazi occupation of Britain, and both of them play on our fear of the worst possible unknown. Jennings concentrates on the grim heroism of his villagers, and merely hints at the presence of the Germans – by their broadcasts (usually preceded by Siegfried's Funeral March), by the occasional guard, or, once, by corpses found on a mountain track. He trades on our fear without undermining our confidence. The village and its inhabitants are destroyed, yet life is shown to renew itself. Well, that seems to be the gist of the subject . . . But, as so often, I find it hard to define sharply the things Jennings stands for. Is Lidice recreated in Wales because he was unable to go to Czechoslovakia? Or is his theme the noble false one that cultures can be oppressed but not destroyed? Or is he merely praising courage? . . . Even so, in spite of these reservations, Jennings does have a belief in something, however vague it may be – and this something brings grandeur to his shots of desolate snow-laden churchyards and haunting castle ruins.

Presumably Brownlow and Mollo also intended to make an anti-Nazi film; but in effect *It Happened Here* is nihilistic. In the final scene a group of English partisans shoot down some English soldiers who are collaborating with the Germans. All notions of national identity have collapsed, and men kill each other without purpose. Yet the directors appear to be quite casual about this ghoulish conclusion, so that we are left wondering whether they underestimate the force of their film, or the value they set on life. *It Happened Here* presents the obverse to the idealism of *The Silent Village*; and the question is, which of them is closer to the truth? Brownlow and Mollo might answer that since Britain was never invaded we can never know. True: all the same, I find that Jennings has the more robust and persuasive attitude; it covers a greater range of experience, it has the power of growth. The things Jennings loved could withstand, and indeed were strengthened by, the challenge of the forces that undermine, ravage and destroy.

And the privy admonishers of men/ Call for fires in the City . . . Jennings was addicted to the poetry of Blake, and above all loved this passage from the *Song of Los*. In *A Man Without a Mask*, Jacob Bronowski* claims that Blake was writing here about both the French Wars *and* the Industrial Revolution. Blake's feelings, says Bronowski, were mixed; he found the Tigers of Wrath and Los, the maker of machines, both admirable and appalling. Jennings also was unable to dissociate the influence of war from the social condition of Britain – and saw the Industrial Revolution as being as much of a threat to his green and pleasant land as a possible German invasion. And like Blake, he was both impressed and shocked by these threats.

As a propagandist, Jennings had one quality both Eisenstein and Riefenstahl lacked: pity. Again and again he shows us how his sympathy lies with the beleaguered, the vulnerable and the destroyed. His portrait of Germany at the end of the war, *A Defeated People* (1945), has some eloquent images of towering ruins. But Jennings is mainly concerned with human misery: children starve, old women lurk in basements, refugees seek for lost members of their families. We are given all the corrosive, sullen despair of the defeated. For once the commentary is dry, factual and uncondescending; it bruises the victors' pride. Yes, we think, it might have happened to us . . .

And yet – it must be stressed – Jennings drew life from the Tigers of Wrath. He filmed while London burned. How exquisite are those blazing warehouses, against which dangling bodies and ladders are seen in silhouette! And Jennings was fascinated by the Industrial Revolution, by its mines and factories and railways – indeed by all kinds of machinery. He finds beauty in melancholic collieries, in the dawn shift, in

---

* In his obituary on Jennings, Bronowski refers to a conversation in which he and Jennings exchanged ideas on Blake and found their points of view remarkably similar.

the discovery of a coal seam beneath the sea. He takes pleasure in the natural sciences, with the self-absorption of a zealot. Sometimes this enthusiasm doesn't transmit to the screen. *The Cumberland Story* (1947), for instance, may tell us a great deal about coal mining, but like its subject is seldom more than a bore. For years Jennings worked on a treatise concerning the relationship of science and poetry in the eighteenth and nineteenth centuries, which remained unfinished at the time of his death in 1952. It was called *Pandemonium* – and in a sense it is true that Jennings did at times lodge uneasily in the capital of Hell, with Satan and his peers.

These literary allusions are, I am afraid, necessary to an understanding of Jennings' work. Jennings read English with I. A. Richards at Cambridge, and was of the same generation as Bronowski, William Empson, and Kathleen Raine – who said of him, 'in that world, we all felt that Humphrey Jennings' was the most remarkable mind we had ever encountered.' I must admit that if this is so, the remarkable mind didn't fulfil itself in the cinema, however good Jennings' films may be. Possibly he dissipated his talents. He painted, wrote verse and prepared a thesis (unfinished) on Thomas Gray, besides thinking about the relationship of science to poetry. Or, possibly, Jennings' talents were not so much dissipated as at war with themselves: an addiction to Blake seems hardly compatible with a liking for Gray and a respect for the methods of science. But if there was an internal conflict, Jennings did his best to conceal it. Already at Cambridge he was – man of his time – against doctrines of personal expression. In both his painting and poetry, says Miss Raine, he sought inspiration in photographs and existing phrases, and not in Nature. He appears to have been ideally prepared for the cinema, above all for the documentary; and, almost inevitably, in 1934 he joined the Crown Film Unit. But his doctrine of impersonality wasn't to fledge until a little later, when he became a member of Charles Madge's Mass Observation Movement.

It is hard now to see why this Movement caused such a stir

in the mid-thirties. In general, the literary people – and, oddly, film critics such as Dilys Powell and George Stonier – were against it. Stonier saw the Mass Observer as someone with 'a loping walk, elephant ears, (and) an eye trained to keyholes.' W. H. Auden dismissed him more harshly in a broadcast as 'a spy, and should be treated as such.' In spite of these attacks, the Mass Observation documents were, and are, still valuable – none more so than the *12th May 1937 Survey*, of which Madge and Jennings were editors-in-chief. This *Survey* is a compilation of a number of responses to the Coronation; and its interest for us is that its technique anticipates in a number of ways the technique Jennings was to use later in his documentaries.

Mass Observation schooled Jennings in the disciplines of science. He observed, contrasted, drew his conclusions meticulously. Later he was to rely on filming the real thing. He never faked his information on the pretext that the imagination can see more deeply than the disinterested eye; even now his material is sometimes taken out of context and shown in newsreels. It is also true that twenty-five years after the Battle of Britain, his war films are completely lacking in nostalgia. This is the Battle as though it were being fought today. In comparison, the magnificent BBC-TV First World War series of 1964 seems blurred in effect, despite its scale and its care for detail. Occasionally one of Jennings' commentaries – seldom written by him – may seem false; the visual side never does. And Jennings' integrity helped him to surmount the self-consciousness of class difference – that pox of the thirties that disfigures even its best documentary, Basil Wright's *Night Mail* (1935).

But the *12th May 1937 Survey* also gives us a lead to the source of Jennings' poetry. 'The celebrations were inescapable; people who tried to avoid them found themselves going back to the radio on one ground or another, or showing a sense of guilt, or found themselves interested after all . . . At a time of dramatic national consciousness the public's propensity for fantasy is strongly stimulated, and gets caught up into connection with the central symbolism.' So runs the commentary, typically self-effacing. But slipped in between the prosaic facts about the Coronation programme and the first group of reports – and possibly inserted by Jennings – is Henry V's soliloquy, 'And what art thou, idol ceremony?' The point of such a ceremony may well be questioned, but its impact cannot be denied. *'Délire officiel d'une grande ville,'* wrote Baudelaire, *'pour troubler le cerveau du solitaire le plus fort.'*

The *Survey* doesn't try to resolve the mystery beyond offering us a hypothesis (from *Totem and Taboo*) of why 'no generation is capable of concealing its more important psychic processes from the next . . .' One of the Mass Observation reports is from an atheist who tried to cut himself off from all public activity on the day of the Coronation, but couldn't help beginning it by wryly anointing his head with hair oil. Whatever we may feel about them, such customs, ceremonies and laws are lodged within us; and Jennings' talent lies in making us acknowledge their force. In spite of ourselves he draws us in, persuades us, moves us. He was a poet of these psychic processes; and his one concern – says Miss Raine – was to express 'the collective symbols of England.' It is clear that Jennings' patriotism, so closely linked with even more primal feelings, is *sacramental* – a mystery that refuses to be explained away. The dome of St Paul's rides against a burning sky . . . When Jennings does try to be explicit, his films sag; the throb of feeling dies, and a false rhetoric takes over.

One curious fact emerging from this survey seems to have had a considerable influence on him. The Coronation brought people together and gave them a feeling of national unity; but at the same time it heightened, by contrast, their chronic sense of isolation. The form of *Listen to Britain* echoes its theme – that the 'music of Britain at war' is like the 'beat of a heart'. But this form brings out also the differences in Britain of culture and class. The placing together of country and seaside, of provincial town and capital city gives us an exaggerated impression of Britain's immensity – much as the hubbub of the dance hall emphasizes the loneliness of the air-raid wardens on the promenade. This contrast doesn't appear in the war films alone. *Spare Time* (1937), which was filmed in Bolton (one of the locations for the first *Survey*), is made up of a number of finely woven impressions of working mens' hobbies: cycling, soccer, whippet racing, pigeon-breeding, brass bands and choirs. 'Spare time – a time most to be ourselves.' Yet the glare of fairground lights makes more desolate the surrounding in- dustrial landscape; the choir chanting Handel deepens the poignancy of the lonely figure in the monotonous street. This melancholy spreads like damp: how strident and grotesque the street band seems as it plays the National Anthem, with its selfconscious Miss Britannia and its gaffers wearing union-jack waistcoats.

All the same, *Spare Time* is no documentary of the fifties; we are closer in spirit to the pageant in Virginia Woolf's *Between the Acts*, than to John Osborne's *The Entertainer*. The artist still has the confidence to express – obliquely maybe – a noble vision of England. We see how things have changed since then when we look at Lindsay Anderson's study of the Covent Garden Market, *Every Day except Christmas* (1957). Anderson is the one person in the British cinema with a temperament at all similar to Jennings'; and yet by the necessity of passing time and changing fashion his range is more limited. *Every Day* opens on a mushroom farm in Sussex. Midnight, and the vegetable lorries, now loaded, move down deserted arterial roads to London. Through the windscreen we see monotonous rows of houses. Above us pass fluorescent lamps. On the radio the Light Programme comes to an end, and the National Anthem plays. Yes, even these mean streets can be redeemed . . . Anderson's intention is noble; yet to his chagrin audiences took it to be satirical. Later in the film we find ourselves in an all- night cafeteria adjacent to the market, where down-and-outs congregate. Anderson films these people with great tenderness – an old sleeping woman, a man with haunted eyes and nico- tine-stained fingers. Then he cuts to the market and tracks along open crates of daffodils, ready for the buyers. It is hard to explain why this contrast is so effective. The daffodils are beautiful, yet remote from the people in the cafeteria who are lost, purposeless, divided against themselves. We are close to the world of Pinter. Social coherence appears to be lost here, and Blake's vision of a green and pleasant land has no place.

However, even in more propitious times, Jennings could run into trouble with his collective symbolism. Some of his non-war films misfire totally. In *S.S. Ionian* (1939) he uses the pretext of a cargo ship's last voyage to hammer out the theme that Britannia rules the waves. Maybe morale needed raising in 1939, but the S.S. Ionian was hardly the boat to carry such a cargo. A mention of Aboukir Bay is enough for Jennings to remind us that here 'Nelson smashed Napoleon's fleet a hundred years ago.' A sequence in Alexandria Harbour allows him to give us a reassuring glimpse of the Mediterranean fleet. This plugging is liable to arouse despair rather than hope. The same is true of *Dim Little Island* (1949), which is a dim little attempt to stir people into exporting more. The times were bad, and Jennings thrashed about to find a theme to redeem them. But he took great risks. By calling on his audience's feelings when his own were not engaged, he debased his currency. As Lindsay Anderson wrote of Jennings' last film,* 'His symbols in *Family Portrait* (1951) – the Long Man of Wilmington, Beachy Head, the mythical horse of Newmarket – what do they really mean to us? Exquisitely presented though it is, the England of this film is nearer to "This England" of the pre-war advertisements and of Mr Castleton Knight's coronation film than to the murky and undecided realities of today.'

I wish Jennings had been more influenced by Blake, who tended to create symbols out of himself, rather than to seek them in popular culture. Even in his finest work, the limitations of collective symbolism are plain. *The Fires Were Started* (1943) describes the activities of the National Fire Service. Barrett, a new recruit (played by the novelist William Sansom), arrives

* Sight and Sound, April 1954.

at the depot; the men prepare for the blitz; the raids start and they fight a warehouse fire. One of them is killed, and the film ends with his funeral. This narrative is weighed down with literary associations. In the dormitory one of the men reads aloud Raleigh's 'O eloquent, just and mighty Death' speech, and also, with little point, Macbeth's 'Ay, in the catalogue ye go for men.' These touches are crude; less so is the well-known sequence in which Barrett plays 'one man went to mow' on the piano and the various firemen, putting on their equipment, enter the room one after the other and join in the round. This sequence is, perhaps, too contrived to stand up to passing time. But I am still moved by a similar moment later on, when the bombs start falling, and Barrett, competing with the noise, thumps out gaily the blues theme of 'Please Don't Ask About Me When I'm Gone.'

In fact, the whole film comes alive as soon as the bombs start to fall. Jennings' control lessens, and all sorts of odd perceptions creep in: the runaway horse (as romantic an effect as anything in Wajda), the backchat and jesting around the all-night canteen van, the woman telephonist answering the phone phlegmatically while wiping blood from her forehead, the cripple picking his way down a dawn street. The action becomes lyrical and enchanted, the editing delicate. But at the fireman's funeral we are once more brought up against the brick wall of collective symbolism. Feeling drains away and, at a loss, we find ourselves asking what the funeral is supposed to represent – Nobility of Sacrifice, Mourning for the National Dead? It all seems out of character with the cockney bonhomie, the casual anti-heroism, of the fire-fighting. We have lost touch with the firemen, and we have no idea what might be going on in their minds. At such moments Jennings' symbolism becomes municipal art, the carvings on a War Memorial frieze. And at such moments we remember the things Jennings excludes; how he ignores the London of, say, black-marketeers and eccentrics, of slackers and the less-than-courageous. Even the most sublime propaganda looks rigidly official when compared to the more personal, more idiosyncratic work of art. Think of Henry Green's novel about the National Guard, *Caught*, with its brilliant portrait of the unstable Pye – or of William Sansom's own account of the period, the short story *Fireman Flower* whose solipsism and insights (such as the fire being 'a fluid abstraction of hot golden light') are at the furthest remove from Jennings' impersonality; or even of Evelyn Waugh's 'group of progressive novelists, in fireman's uniform, squirting a little jet of water into the morning-room' – and one begins to see what Jennings misses out.

But perhaps I am just carping. Rhetoric always has its price – and Jennings' rhetoric is often worth the cost, as we can see from *A Diary for Timothy* (1945), with its script by E. M. Forster. Jennings had a number of affinities to Forster besides an allegiance to Cambridge. 'Only connect', for instance, could well describe his driving impulse. 'When peace comes, don't forget the land and its people again,' claims the commentary to *Spring Offensive* (1940). The countryside and the cities are part of one another, inseparable; the boundaries are much further beyond. Jennings is always eager to point out connections and to show how decisions are reached in the committee room – and in this way, as in others, he helped establish the style of the television documentary. Often his committee scenes are visually gauche (amateur actors don't help) and ill-married to the sensitive Romantic filming of neglected farms at dawn. But Jennings is too honest to leave them out.

It may appear strained to associate the diffident Forster with rhetoric or propaganda; then we remember Forster's vision of the 'unseen pressing on the seen' – as clumsy as anything in Jennings:

'Does (England) belong to those who have moulded her and made her feared by other lands, or to those who have added nothing to her power, but have somehow seen her, seen the whole island at once, lying as a jewel in a silver sea, sailing as a ship of souls, with all the brave world's fleet accompanying her towards eternity?' (*Howards End.*)

There are moments when the commentary to *A Diary for Timothy* (read by Michael Redgrave) goes perilously close to the verge of self-parody, as the cast of *Beyond the Fringe* affectionately made plain – such moments as when we see Myra Hess playing a piece by Beethoven, and the narrator reminds us that this music was written by a German, and that it's the Germans we are fighting now: 'After the war, we'll have to think that one out.' But these moments of bathos are few (the narrator is supposed to be avuncular anyway), and the general tenor of the film is one of caution. Forster and Jennings, indeed, collaborate admirably. Forster's script is typically Forsterian; yet it allows Jennings to develop freely the ideas and associational techniques of *Listen to Britain*.

In structure *A Diary for Timothy* weaves its themes around five characters: the infant Timothy; a wounded bed-ridden pilot, Peter Roper, as much at the mercy of others as is the infant; a miner, Gyronwy, injured while cutting coal; a farmer, and an engine driver. Of these characters the infant, the pilot and the miner are the most important, and it is by relating their personal situation to the progress and significance of the war that the film is given direction. The complacent warm world of the newborn child is contrasted with the pain and weariness of the last months of the war and with fearful hopes for the future. The tragedy of Arnhem takes place and the muddy foggy days of mid-winter close in. During this grim time Gyronwy is injured in the mines; and the point is made, more explicitly than ever before, that the legacy of the Industrial Revolution is almost as dangerous as a possible German invasion. Again and again, the camera comes back to the infant – 'It's a chancy world, Timothy.' And yet, though Timothy is lucky, the comforts of his Rectory home are threatened. Gradually the central theme of the *Diary* emerges. The war is being fought, not merely to defeat the aggressors but to make a more just world, where Gyronwy's kind of accident is less likely to occur. From a historian's viewpoint, *A Diary for Timothy* is a wonderful illustration of why Britain went Labour in 1945.

Yet the film doesn't follow the straight and narrow of a good thesis. Like *Listen to Britain* it moves in waves, pulling in more and more associations. It resembles an incoming tide that draws back only in order to sweep further forward. As always, the device of news bulletins is put to fine use: at Arnhem, the announcer tells us, men caught water in their capes – and this phrase 'men caught water in their capes' becomes a refrain beautifully repeated as we are shown dripping water butts in London. Bombed houses are related to slums in Glasgow and to the ruins of Warsaw, and to all the desolation of that winter. Then Christmas and hope – and one of the most poignant moments in the film, poignant maybe because unintended. Jennings was a radical, and he wanted to change society. Many of the changes he looked forward to have come about; but in ways he didn't appear either to foresee or want. For he was a traditionalist in sentiment, and the *Diary* is his most overtly religious film in its affirmation of the Christmas spirit – the cosy Rectory, the drinking of toasts, the Christmas tree and the carols – all those customs which the new world Jennings wished for has diminished rather than strengthened.

But he was not to know this. The seasons change. New Year brings rimy, clear weather, and as the camera rises from a view of a frozen river to a lovely winter landscape, a boys' choir sings *Adeste Fidelis*. The news from the Front improves; Peter Roper and Gyronwy begin to recover; and Timothy gurgles in his pram. Perhaps Jennings rather overstresses this change for the better, or perhaps we feel it overstressed because we are embarrassed now to be reminded of the 'glorious Russian offensive' of that time. Anyhow, this burst of hope and excitement is soon dampened down – 'it's a chancy world.' Gyronwy, recovering in a stately home, looks up at a Tiepoloesque ceiling and wonders whether the old days of the thirties, of unemployment and starvation, will recur when the war is over.

The war ends – and the narrator warns us that life will become more dangerous, since now we have the power to choose and criticize. The *Diary* is only about war ostensibly; its central figure is an infant, and its main concern is with the future – where do we go from here? . . . 'I think beach-combing is in my line,' says Roper as he rejoins his squadron for the final offensive (a delicious moment, this, for all connoisseurs of the forties). Nothing is certain: mines blow up on beaches, while scenes from Gielgud's *Hamlet* ('Alas, poor Yorick!') are interposed with moments in a canteen, presently blitzed.

Jennings embodied contradictions peculiar to the English temperament. He was a republican who needed the monarchy, a socialist who believed in the most conservative symbols of England, a Romantic who followed the most severe doctrines of impersonality.

Fritz Lang

(The German Period: 1919-33)

'Mythopoeia is a far more common characteristic of the human race (and especially of the German race) than veracity.'

H. Trevor-Roper—*The Last Days of Hitler*

Professor Trevor-Roper rightly mocks at Nazi superstition and at its paranoid attempt to dissolve the world into a lurid delusion: yet mythopoeia and veracity are not necessarily opposed. One of the reasons why Fritz Lang's German films have been so long undervalued, I would suggest, is that they are held to be myths of this type – Nazi lies, rather than disturbed reflections of their time.

There are at least three ways in which a myth can reveal truth: by the vividness of its central image – and this vividness depends on the extent to which the image gathers up some aspect of common experience; by such formal qualities as harmony and complexity; and by its conveyed sense of moral discovery. At his best Lang (aided by his script-writing wife, Thea von Harbou) creates myths that fulfil all these requirements. No one has evolved a more telling image of the modern city. Few German artists have conveyed the difficulties of the post-war era so honestly, so naively, so undogmatically – though Lang would understandably disclaim the title of 'artist'; it was one Hitler liked to use of himself. At the beginning, his films trace the confusion and anxieties of the Weimar Republic. Later they dally with an easy persuasive solution to these problems. And yet Lang's flirtation with National Socialism is no more than a flirtation. In 1931 he made 'M' (working title, *Murderer*

85

Among Us), and in 1932 *The Testament of Dr Mabuse*: both films explicitly reject the Nazi solution.

In fact, these films make a far more valuable political document than, say, the impoverished myths of the young Eisenstein, with all their pretensions to historical truth. Lang never sets out to nail down a 'social problem' – some situation so abstracted, mulled over and attenuated that it can be reduced to a slogan. Nor does he thrust his material at us as though it were a tract. It is hard to believe now that many critics once considered the greatest 'art' film of the twenties to be *Battleship Potemkin*. But then, as Siegfried Kracauer knows, the most persuasive way to sell right-thinking films is to make claims for their artistic merit and to pretend the propaganda doesn't exist. (You reverse the procedure for wrong-thinking ones.)

Kracauer is an appropriate person to mention in this context since no one has done more damage to Lang's reputation than he has, in his *From Caligari to Hitler* (1947). In this study, Kracauer tries to demonstrate how the German cinema unwittingly encouraged the political climate that led to Hitler by a *post hoc, ergo propter hoc* description of the films. His thesis appears to have had a widespread influence; yet it doesn't stand up to much questioning. (To apply Kracauer's method: imagine what film historians would have made of *Public Enemy* and *Scarface* if the United States had turned Fascist in 1940.) The most debatable part of this book is the section devoted to Lang. Kracauer handles the films in a summary fashion; he is less interested in them than in attacking their maker. To say the least, Kracauer gives the impression of carrying on a personal feud. But maybe he has good reason for feeling resentment – even he must be aware of how Lang is the exception which makes nonsense of his thesis.

But this thesis is already weakened in other ways. Kracauer claims to be analysing films as social documents, yet he doesn't make even one detailed reference to the novel, the theatre or the journalism of the time; he treats the cinema as a purely self-contained activity. In general, his approach is to take certain ideas from *The Cabinet of Dr Caligari* and to trace their development through later films under the blanket term of Expressionism. Now, Lang did make one expressionist film (*Der Müde Tod*) and did at times use expressionist tricks, but what is most striking about his Mabuse series, *Spione*, and 'M' is their idiosyncratic, quite personal blend of fantasy and realism. Lang seldom uses the typical subjective distortions of the Expressionists; he was trained as an architect (his father's profession), and his studio sets are nearly always as solid and real as the world outside.

His films are more than a sum of their visual ideas. In fact, their vigour stems primarily from a non-filmic source – and it is by failing to make the most of this source that Kracauer really misunderstands Lang's achievement. For though he does mention Oswald Spengler twice, his comment on both occasions is in passing; and yet Spengler, I am sure, is the necessary starting point for any understanding of the Langian mythology.

The Decline of the West was published in 1918. Kracauer tells us that responsible critics at once set out to show how the book made nonsense as history, since in this case mythopoeia and veracity *were* opposed. All the same, the book enraptured the German public and became a best-seller. Understandably so; even now Spengler's rhapsody expresses a vision of modern life which, at any rate emotionally, still rings true, nowhere more so than in its chapter on 'The Soul of the City' – the sombre note of which provides a groundbase to Lang's own more elaborate orchestration.

Man is doomed, cries Spengler. When he first takes to the city his intellect is freed and his genius fulfilled. But divorced from Nature he becomes febrile, and his interests grow abstract. The city is like a drug; man cannot escape; gradually he weakens and dies.

'It is the city that first defies the land, contradicts Nature in the lines of its silhouette, denies all Nature . . . And then

87

begins the gigantic megalopolis, the city-as-world, which suffers nothing beside itself ... By day there is a street traffic of strange colours and tones, and by night a new light that outshines the moon ... The notion of money attains to full abstractedness ... It values things, no longer as between each other, but *with reference to itself*. Its relation to the soil and to the man of the soil has so completely vanished, that in the economic thought of the leading cities – the money markets – it is ignored. Money has now become a power and, moreover, a power that is wholly intellectual ...

Man is seized by his own creation, the City, and is made into its creature, its executive organ, and, finally, its victim ... But always the splendid mass harbours lamentable poverty and degraded habits, and the attic and mansards, the cellars and back courts are breeding a new type of raw man ... The wheels of Destiny roll on to its end; the birth of the City entails its death ...

What makes the man of the world-cities incapable of living on any but this artificial footing is that the cosmic beat in his being is ever-decreasing ... Tension without cosmic pulsation to animate it is the transition to nothingness. And Civilization is nothing but tension ... The last man of the world-city no longer wants to live – he may cling to life as an individual, but as a type, as an aggregate, no, for it is a characteristic of this collective existence that it eliminates the terror of death.'

This style is turgid, often silly, its content remote from reality and sometimes potentially vicious – 'money is only overthrown by blood'. But Spengler's romanticism is powerful stuff, and one can see why Lang was stimulated by it. As a starting point, he takes over *en bloc* the ideas of fatality and of the intellect hatching plots wildly as though in a void. But, above all, he is fascinated by the idea of the city. Gradually his idea becomes more rewarding than Spengler's – silhouettes emerge, then dimensions; we begin to see the city as a complex

88

of interests, as a jungle of conflicting appetites, as a symbol (through architecture) of the mind's depths, and (primarily through gadgets) of all forms of magical communication, a construct so delicate that the slightest touch can make it unbalance. And finally, in 'M' and *The Testament*, those last frail bulwarks against the deluge, the city is shown to embody (in spite of all its defects and ways it can be misused) sanity, order and civilization – through the figure of the great detective. Lang (happily) has little time for agrarian mysticism; save for one lapse in *Metropolis*, the good and simple peasant makes no appearance.

But this is to anticipate. *Dr Mabuse – the Gambler* (Part 1. *The great gambler: a picture of the age.* Part 2. *Inferno.*), the four hour epic made in 1922, is still close to Spenglerian themes: a sense of doom, a society enervated by city pleasures, a mastermind controlling and manipulating just about everybody. In 1919, Lang had directed a lengthy serial, *The Spiders*; and *Dr Mabuse* has, formally, much of the serial about it. The plot appears improvised and the narrative inconsequential, sometimes to the point of being cryptic (why, for example, is the title of Goethe's *Götz von Berlichingen* found scribbled on a cell wall in one of the final sequences?). Odd for the serial form, though, is its lack of action: after a brilliantly conceived robbery at the start (brilliantly conceived, that is, by both Lang and Dr Mabuse) the film settles down comfortably to a series of dialogues and arias, only now and then interspersed by some burst of activity. Still, in spite of its shaky development *Dr Mabuse* rivets the attention. Why so?

The reason, I suspect, is not so much Lang's visual style, though this is hypnotic enough, as his (and von Harbou's) strict control over their themes. *Dr Mabuse*, in fact, is a half-designed yet clear blueprint for the taut construction of the later work. The opening shot announces its central theme: a hand of cards, on each of which is superimposed the doctor's face in various disguises. Like all gamblers, Mabuse is faced with a wide range of possibilities – and the nature of gambling being what it is, most of them are liable to boomerang back on him. But Mabuse differs from the ordinary gambler in two ways: his game covers the whole of society, and, since he is a cheat, is usually to his advantage.

Lang keeps to few locations, the greater part of them being gambling dens of one sort or another: the stock exchange, nightclubs, card rooms. In the four hours at his disposal he is able to build up a ferocious picture of a society devoured by its own greed. The air is thick with cigar and cigarette smoke; people inhale desperately as though gasping for breath. The camera pans over a trolley in a restaurant loaded with food, over rows of brandy bottles, over trout in pools waiting to be grilled. The city dwellers are as voracious as sharks, and yet, like the shark, have soft under-bellies, beautifully exposed to the more acute predator.

Mabuse looks a man of high intelligence – noble brow, white locks, piercing eyes. He is played by Lang's favourite actor of this period, Rudolf Klein Rogge (cosily enough, von Harbou's first husband), a great actor in the heroic mould with something of a resemblance to Queen Victoria (or Angus Wilson). Why, then, should this panjandrum wish to use his talents so meanly? Well, Mabuse is a Spenglerian man – a *maudit*, a gambler in the grip of vice. When moral values collapse people resort to superstition; fortune-tellers thrived during the First World War. So Mabuse, a man of his time, clings to the last hope – to gamble against chance. He plays the game hard, with the intensity of despair, with the intensity of a Napoleon making his last stand, or of a nineteenth-century tragedian hamming through five acts. He performs to the hilt, even when, as a drunken *matelot* on his way to inspect his private sweat-shop of counterfeiters, he is alone and unnoticed.

As the opening shot implies, Mabuse gambles in identity. His cards don't make up an ordinary pack but various types of made-up face. He can become an infinite number of people, can dis-

90

solve into all classes, can take on all shapes and guises. Presently, as Mabuse becomes more and more volatile, he loses human identity and becomes no more than a conventional vampire sucking out lives. (Vampire films were in vogue: F. W. Murnau's *Nosferatu*, with a script by the ubiquitous von Harbou, appeared in 1921). Then – another transformation – he becomes less a creature than a metaphysical force, a devil who sits in darkness, 'hatching vain empires'. Finally he seems to become death itself, the most extreme game of chance against which all men eventually lose. Lang had already personified Death as a weary, cloaked traveller in *Der Müde Tod*: but how weak this allegory appears when compared to the fabulous irradiations of the satanic doctor!

Mabuse is all things to all men: everything and nothing. He lives in a house with a beautiful Renaissance portico; he is, in an inverted form, *l'uomo universale*. On a more mundane, though no less grand level, he carries on two professions: psychiatry *and* banking. As one of the earliest of analysts he deploys hypnotism – and so is able to turn others into puppets and to set up a long range control over them. He creeps into their brains and makes them cheat at cards or fall in love with him. His most notable conquest is of two typically Spenglerian city degenerates, dying because they lack the energy to live: the Count and Countess Told – an exquisite, unnatural and rather charmingly distrait couple. (If for nothing else, *Dr Mabuse* can be recommended as an anthology of Romantic attitudes; the count is straight out of Huysman's *À Rebours*). Mabuse soon insinuates himself into the Count's mansion, with its 'decadent' art collection of Oceanic sculpture and Expressionist paintings, and swiftly makes his way into the Countess's bed. (In fact, he seduces her on what appears to be an analyst's couch.) The possession is complete, and we soon see the master-mind preening himself beneath a hideous painting of the devil.

Hypnosis is a form of invisible control – the important fact for

Lang being its invisibility. As *Metropolis* makes plain, his city is both real and magical, a merging of naturalism and legend. The city may be created and maintained by the use of science and technology; but on one level at least, Lang treats science and technology as though they were a form of magic. He plays on the primitive in all of us – the primitive who sees the city, with its telephones, radios and indeed films, as a place of magical (because unseen) communication. Other directors may have been first to realize the potential of such exotic machines as space-craft; but Lang, I believe, was the first one to reveal the magic in ordinary instruments. (The most notable amongst many directors to share such an interest is John Frankenheimer, whose talent for showing politics as a network of almost occult powers, either in its use of gadgets (*Seven Days in May*), or in its manipulation of people – the most extreme example being brainwashing (*The Manchurian Candidate*) – is surely indebted to Lang's example.)

Frankenheimer's work reminds us of how politics can be seen in terms of another form of invisible communication – 'No matter what individual qualities or defects a man may have,' writes Hannah Arendt about Imperialism, 'once he has entered the maelstrom of an unending process of expansion, he will cease to be what he was and obey the laws of the process, and identify himself with the anonymous forces he is supposed to serve in order to keep the whole process in motion.' (*The Origins of Totalitarianism.*) To quote Arendt in the context of *Dr Mabuse* may seem a case of asking an elephant to lift a pea; yet Lang, I feel, is already moving towards an intuitive understanding of her argument. At this stage, though, he is unable to formulate it in terms of plot (as he is by the time of 'M'). He seems to be enjoying the 'uncontrollable forces' – of using their filmic possibilities without grasping what they entail.

Still, he does seem to understand how politics in the Arendtian sense have died in the city. In Mabuse's city political interests have been displaced by social ones. The public sphere has been splintered apart into factions concerned, often secretly, with protecting their private affairs: their property, their tenure over others, their plots to commit crimes. Order, insofar as it exists, is maintained by the police, and in *Dr Mabuse* police authority is precarious. Magic has to be challenged by magic – or so we are led to suppose – and no ordinary detective brings about Mabuse's fall. The Holmesian von Wenk is also a master-mind, only able to destroy this Moriarty by becoming, as it were, his mirror image: he has to work in secrecy, take on disguise, resort to trickery. But such stratagems degrade the notion of justice and public service. Von Wenk is as much a victim of the unending process as Mabuse, and almost to the same extent corrupted. The forces of good as embodied in him are feeble – yet he is the only good in the film, since he alone is capable of stopping the tyrant's rise to total power.

But do such moral judgements, such references to good and evil, apply to a world in madness? Lang, you could argue, is so involved in the devices of gambling and playing that he is unable to stand back and evaluate them; rather, he takes us more and more into the disordered furious world of obsession. Even in madness Count Told continues to play cards – with phantoms. And Mabuse, also driven insane, continues wildly to hatch plots.

'To hatch plots' – the truth of the matter is that in one sense Mabuse is close to being Lang himself – nowhere more plainly so than in one of the final scenes when Mabuse appears before a vast audience as 'Sandor Weltman', psychologist, and carries out a mass hypnosis (much as the cinema is supposed to do), conjuring an oasis and a cohort of Arabs on camelback out of a desert backcloth; Cinerama before its time. In less than the last resort, it is Lang who inhabits Mabuse's elaborate green room, who works the magic and who holds the joker in the pack.

And, indeed, there *is* something magical about his style. The photography of *Dr Mabuse* is often remarkably beautiful, as when the mad count wanders with a candelabra through his twilight mansion, or as when the countess in black flowing robes and wide-brimmed hat confesses her love of the doctor. As for the lighting – well, in that Lang is his own master. He favours middle or long distance shots, and a rim lighting that gives his characters both dimension and solidity, and emboldens our sense of their relationship to room or street. In *Dr Mabuse* rooms tend to be ample, while streets are so narrow that cars jam and bump into each other. Rooms with a twenties setting are few compared to those with Victorian furnishings – ponderous rooms that belie the fantastic events taking place in them. It seems appropriate when one of Mabuse's hirelings blows up von Wenk's office: in microcosm, it seems to repeat the shocking disruption of the past, and the continuing reverberations of the First World War on the pre-1914 mind.

Lang fought in that war. But if you see the Victorian rooms as reflections of the parental home and the doctor's wickedness as no worse than a child's, then Lang's films, you may think, refer to events even more deeply personal. Mabuse rules the city as though it were a nursery, creeping through sewers as though beneath tables, or like Harold Lloyd, clambering over roofs as though they were chairs. There is nothing to fear: the city is his terrain and belongs to him. In reality, the city may be amorphous and menacing; but, for a time at least, Mabuse does allow us to pretend that given his magical/infantile power we too could surpass the possible fear of chaos it arouses in us.

In *Metropolis* (1926) this fear of chaos is also faultily reconciled by magic and, since it makes greater claims on our adult response, to a more grating effect. The metropolis is Spengler's city of the future, a stony phantasmagoria conceived of by Lang on his first view of New York. The city's strata reflect the social order. The rulers live in skyscrapers and airy terraced gardens. The workers (no more than slaves) toil far beneath the ground in factories; their homes are far beneath the factories, in a slum city deep in the earth.

The direction of Lang's sympathy towards these two classes

is uncertain, possibly confused, with the result that he is finally evasive in answering the film's main question of how to resolve this class conflict. The ruling class are as febrile and guilt-ridden as the city dwellers in *Dr Mabuse*, and take their pleasures just as sadly. Freder, dictator of Metropolis, is an endearing intellectual with moist doggy eyes, doomed to carry out a job he cannot control – doomed because, like God, he has no right to abdicate. There is a strong sense of the inevitable; Freder never questions his role, never even thinks of establishing an egalitarian society. Indeed, such issues are never mentioned, let alone discussed, so that we never really feel him to be responsible for the cruelty or the injustice of his city. Meanwhile, the workers are seen as pitiful broken creatures, heads bowed as they shuffle to work. In the great engine rooms they pull at heavy levers or move pistons automatically, monotonously, and without pause until, worn out, they die. Lang's vision of the oppressed is powerful – all the more so now with our hindsight knowledge of the concentration camps. *Metropolis* is Lang's first attempt to trade, in his masterly fashion, on our sense of fear.

But this play on our emotions is suspect. Granted, Lang is dealing with a social problem indirectly; still, however indirectly, the social problem is there, and Lang distorts it grossly by the way in which he turns it into mythology. Young Freder's vision of the machines as Moloch, a gaping steaming mouth, or Maria's vision of the Tower of Babel are even more stupendous than Griffith's Fall of Babylon; as visual effects they have seldom, if ever, been equalled in the cinema. The three seemingly infinite processions of slaves converging into the centre of the screen, the great stairs – a familiar idea in Lang's work – and the tower itself, as fabulous as the City of Worms in *Siegfried*, all these glow in the memory. And yet, to see man-devouring machines as symbols of destiny and death, however awe-struck our response, is to simplify (as in *Modern Times*) an urgent problem that at that time cried out for an honest solution. In this context to blame machines was as good as to whitewash the record of dictators and bureaucrats. In the twenties *Metropolis*, I suspect, did a great deal of harm to its audiences, and I can understand why H. G. Wells dismissed it as 'plain silly'.

In another way also Lang plays, maybe unintentionally, on our natural conservatism; he writes a religious allegory into his plot. Freder has a son so obtuse that he has failed, even though he is in his mid-twenties, to learn the reasons for his father's power. One day a girl named Maria and a group of the workers' children enter his pleasure garden (a place for orgies and such-like). Pointing to the children Maria says, 'Look at these your brothers' – and a social conscience is born. Freder Jnr follows her down into the abyss and for the first time sees the engine rooms. He is appalled. When one of the workers collapses he takes over; but the machines soon crucify him. 'Oh father, father,' he cries, 'I didn't know ten hours could be such torture.' Maria is a quietist missionary (sent by Whom?) who preaches to the workers before an altar in a catacomb lit by candles. (She is Lang's one lapse towards agrarian mysticism.) When young Freder appears at one of these meetings, the infatuated Maria proclaims him to be the long-awaited saviour – the man who, in Maria's words, is the heart that mediates between arm and brain. Her decision is calamitous, since it forces Freder Snr into the vicious, underhand reprisal of flooding the workers' city. All comes out well in the end, though, when the young saviour and Maria are united beneath the thoughtful benediction of his father, in a courageous synthesis of the Christian and Oedipal myths. Industry comes to terms with itself in the portico of the cathedral: Freder Snr shakes hands with the leading workers' representative (in fact, one of his own spies); the heart, as it were, mediates between arm and brain. It is worth remembering that this compromise, this sham ending, of which Lang is ashamed, was much admired by Hitler. (According to Lang, Goebbels told him that, 'many years before, he and the Führer had seen my *Metropolis* in a small town, and Hitler had said at the time that he wanted me to run the Nazi film industry.')

This reconciliation is possible because the devil has been exorcized; the devil in this case being the inventor Redwort (Klein Rogge). Redwort is a hunchback with an iron hand, and like the dwarfs in *Siegfried* is clearly to be despised as sub-Aryan. He is also a scientist, which in Langian terms means someone as subversive as a magician. He is the inventor of the machines, the true creator of Metropolis – even capable of constructing a robot so skilfully in imitation of Maria that it incites the workers to Luddism. In short, Redwort is a scape-goat, whose Hunchback of Notre Dame conflict with Freder Jnr on the parapets of the cathedral ends with his inevitable fall to death.*

Metropolis remains one of the most vivid of Lang's films, a continuous source of inspiration; it is also one of his least attractive. In *Siegfried* he could get away with his blond beast, epitome of German youth; the myth made no claims to veracity. But *Metropolis* purports to be close to the actual – and on such a level the best I can say for it is that it successfully disproves the cruder forms of the commitment theory: as it shows, the aesthetic quality of a film need not be entirely judged by the value of its political judgements.

Shortly after *Metropolis* came the turning point, for in 1932 Lang made 'M', his first film to call fully on our response as adults, and which uses the boys' own brilliance of the earlier work to stir our deepest feelings. Its plot is based on the case of the Düsseldorf child murderer, Peter Kürsten, and is devised to show how one frightened little man is able, unsuspectingly, to disrupt the entire mechanism of a city. To some extent, then, it is a grotesque comedy – but this comedy is held in check,

* A scientist with an iron hand, a doom-laden situation in which doom is equated with the inexorable power of machines, an office with flashing bulbs and huge maps – the association seems inevitable; and yet no one, so far as I know, has pointed out how Stanley Kubrick's *Dr Strangelove* is indebted to *Metropolis*.

and not allowed to diminish the tragic element. The first shot is of children playing in a courtyard: the camera pans to mothers on tenement landings talking to each other and to their children below; the last shot is of a chorus, three mothers in mourning at the Murderer's trial, saying, 'And if he dies, will it bring back our children?' The comedy of the city, its confusions and violence, is measured against this pain of loss.

You could see 'M' as a graph of Lang's own development, since many of its ironies play round the conflict between the infantile and the adult. The death of children, made all the more poignant by their remaining toys, or the toys used to seduce them, is contrasted with the Murderer, doomed to remain emotionally like a child. Lang develops his usual theme of fatality without, happily, his usual relish: the Murderer's great confession to the criminals, in which he pleads to being unlike them in the sense that he has no choice but must murder, and of how he is always afraid of the unknown inner forces that can possess him, is in substance commonplace now. But in 1932 it must have been electrifying – and the film still conveys this excitement. Also, the speech is played by Peter Lorre, whose Murderer, ever gobbling or rolling his eyes like a plump and pimply toad, remains a classic amongst screen performances. 'M' anticipates such American films as Lang's *Fury* or *Scarlet Street* in so far as much of the time we see the action through the eyes of the exploited rather than the exploiter – as much through the eyes of Count Told as of Mabuse.

'I am always afraid of myself': such is the principal theme. The murders stir up a murderous element in most of the inhabitants of the city. We enter a time of panic, almost insanity, in which good and bad are hopelessly intertwined. Everyone suspects everybody else. A timid elderly man needs merely talk to a girl by a tram-stop and a threatening mob arises round him. Witnesses quarrel. No one observes, no one remembers – and, anyway, it all happened so long ago. Perceptions are doubted; evidence is ambiguous; things are seen through mirrors and windows. Officials fulminate, phone each other and write letters to little effect. The blind lead the blind, so that, not unexpectedly, the first useful clue as to the nature of the murderer is given by a blind balloon-seller.

Above all, this grotesque comedy conditions the sub-plot. The police, under pressure to discover the murderer, round up criminals and raid their dens; the underworld is disrupted, ordinary business is out of the question. So the criminals gang together in a determination to take justice into their own hands and to hunt down the killer themselves – a parody of Justice in the manner of Brecht's *The Threepenny Opera* (1928). The criminals organize themselves with a bourgeois propriety, and their leader echoes bourgeois sentiments: 'This beast has no right to exist'. At times, as they sit round a table smoking furiously, they unknowingly resemble a police conference. Smoking people create their own fog. The more they smoke and think and speculate, the more cloudy things become. But in fact criminals remain criminals, and when they do track down the Murderer and round him up they remind us less of the traditional bourgeoisie than of the Nazis; instead of the cruelty (or smugness) of indifference, we have a realized sadism.

At first this sadism throbs beneath the surface, as the criminals (disguised as beggars) patrol the city. Relationships are, it seems, poisoned by their gaze; a 'blind' man's scrutiny appears to contaminate the spontaneous chat of a mother and child. But this sadism becomes painfully obvious as soon as the Murderer becomes a marked man; that is, when one of the beggars presses a chalk mark 'M' on the back of his jacket. Gradually the Murderer realizes he is being watched. There is an extraordinary cat-and-mouse scene, reminiscent of Kirilov's suicide in *The Possessed*, when, finding himself trapped at a cross-road, he comes face to face with one of his persecutors. They stare at each other for a long moment; then the Murderer starts running and the chase begins. The criminals hound him down to a furniture depository, where he locks himself into a room loaded with junk. Finally, when caught, he is taken to a mock-trial in a ruined brewery, and is virtually lynched by the mob.

99

Lang once said that he lives through his eyes; and it is true that in *Dr Mabuse* his images of hierarchy, of the heights and depths, is principally confined to the spatial: to buildings, to the various levels of the city, to the play of light and dark. In *Metropolis* these images are extended to take in the conflict between the adult and infantile parts of the mind. In 'M' the stress on the irrational is even more marked and frequent. Terror is palpable, yet its source is unknown. There is a disparity between act and motive (hence the grotesque comedy). The criminals are more systematic in their violence than the workers in *Metropolis*, yet they act on a slender, almost whimsical pretext. Irrationality reigns, and the lord of misrule is the Murderer. Though his function in the film's structure is similar to Mabuse's, he is more real as a person and so more convincing. He is far from being a superior intellect, far from giving the impression of controlling the action – is merely a lodger in a dismal bedsitter.

But the reign of irrationality doesn't last. Indeed no film disproves Kracauer's thesis more trenchantly. To all appearances, certainly, the city turns into a panic-ridden place, hit by inflation as well as the murder scare (again, the disparity of motive and action). Its accumulation of objects – the criminals' loot, the paraphernalia of dossiers and finger-prints, the stacks of food – arouse despair in us since they are so unending. But, we also despair at its state of being a continual prison – a place of locked doors and barred windows. The junk room in the depository where the Murderer is trapped admirably brings together this contrast between meaningless disorder and confinement.

Seemingly, panic brings on a general loss of identity. Individuals are submerged into groups – into being criminals, the police or the mob. Not to ally yourself with a group is to risk becoming a scapegoat. As panic first grips the city, the police raid a thieves' den and hold an identity-card check. One man, having no card, tries to make an unsuccessful escape through a barred window. But there is another man who never needs to escape and who never loses his identity – Lohman, the police inspector.

According to Kracauer, Lohman is a 'colourless official'. Nothing is further from the truth. Though under extreme pressure from public opinion and his superiors this formidable hero never loses his nerve; nor does he waver in his knowledge of what is right or wrong. He may seem paternal and tolerant to the criminals, but in fact he misses nothing and makes no concessions. Under his command the police work diligently; even without the criminals' inside knowledge they are virtually as quick as them in tracing down the Murderer and bringing him to a just trial. At the end, whatever Kracauer may claim, the city's order is restored.

Lohman's ebullience, you could say, is reflected in Lang's brisk style of narrative. There is no gloating over chaos (as in *Dr Mabuse*), no pleasure in the murders or the hunt. The thematic editing through newspapers, letters and dossiers, or the juxtaposition of such incongruities as an ordinary finger print followed by one blown up to screen size, or the vivid contrast between kinds of lighting, anticipate the bravura shorthand style of *Citizen Kane*. The urgency of this pace underlines the tragedy of loss – 'And if he dies, will it bring back our children?' Lohman is like a beacon that brings comfort and yet makes the surrounding night seem darker.

In this sense, I cannot overstress his importance; he is more than a link-man between 'M' and *The Testament of Dr Mabuse*. W. H. Auden (amongst others) has described the thriller as a form of debased theology. Lang, like Chesterton in *The Man Who Was Thursday*, tries to polish this tarnished pedigree by turning the thriller into a metaphysical allegory. Tired of his satanic doctor, Lang was only interested in making a sequel on the off-chance of being able (he claims) to subvert Nazi propaganda. In fact, his criticism of the Nazis is veiled, but as much by other interests creeping in as by caution. *The Testament* is a continuation of *Dr Mabuse – the Gambler* with the insane

Mabuse now confined to an asylum, scribbling out his plans and covering the cell floor with sheets upon sheets of paper. But Mabuse soon dies; and his soul transmigrates into the body of his superintendent, the psychiatrist Professor Baum, and forces him to organize plots which, in theory, should allow Mabuse's gang to disrupt the country and come to power. Lang's image of the city is extended: to the familiar ironies of criminals becoming judges, of psychologists becoming lunatics, of lunatics becoming despots, and of the hunter being hunted, is added a further concourse as the world of the dead begins to interfuse with the world of the living.

Lohman soon discovers that 'all clues lead to the asylum'. All the world is a prison, and prisons can become madhouses: so runs Lang's attack on the Nazis. But stone walls don't make an absolute prison; a soul can transmigrate from one body into another or suddenly appear in a locked room. The world is a cypher and the key has been lost; even bare rooms are enigmas waiting to be read by some supra-natural power. *The Testament* opens on an empty cellar. Lamps sway, and on a worktable bottles rattle. The camera pans over these moving objects slowly, as though wishing to probe into the cause of their mysterious agitation; a thunderous roar, presumably from an engine-room nearby, doesn't appear to be an adequate explanation. The hand of Hofmeister, a police spy, obtrudes from behind a trunk . . . Hofmeister eventually manages to escape from the building to be assaulted by unseen forces. A falling rock grazes him, blazing petrol cans thunder towards him along the pavement. Presently he is found mad and in the dark, crooning a meaningless ditty.

Mabuse's (and later Professor Baum's) gang don't know who their employer might be. When this employer wishes to give them orders he summons them by telecom to a bare room, half curtained off, and speaks to them from behind the curtain. Amongst the hirelings is Kent, a murderer reformed by his girl Lille, who is exasperated by some of these orders. Eventually he loses his temper and shoots at the curtain. But behind it he finds no one – merely a table, an amplifier and a metal silhouette (remarkably similar to Lang's). The two lovers are imprisoned in this room and warned by amplifier that they will shortly be blown up. They strip wallpaper off a doorway and find the door blocked. Their last hope, thanks to an exposed pipe, is to flood the room and to let water cushion them against the blast. The water rises and drives them into a corner, lifting the amplifier off the table and floating it round them pointedly in a slow arc... At the same time Mabuse's gang are trying to shoot their way out of a barricaded flat elsewhere, having failed to drill an exit through the ceiling.

In effect, we are back to Lang's interest in communication, either when it takes magical forms – through machines such as gramophones and amplifiers, hypnosis, and (more extremely) transmigration – or when it breaks down, so that things turn into riddles or enigmas. After the attempt on his life, Hofmeister tries to get in touch with Lohman by phone; but the busy inspector orders his assistant to tell Hofmeister that he is dead. He learns too late that Hofmeister holds valuable information concerning the recent crime wave: by then the spy is mad, and not even the Inspector's trick of pretending to repeat the phone call (using the alarm on his watch as a ringing bell) can pierce Hofmeister's arrested mind. All clues may lead to the madhouse, but how is the sane mind to interpret them? Nothing is what it seems in this fantastic world of continual transformations: at the end of the film Professor Baum tries to murder Hofmeister in his cell, but by some mysterious process goes mad himself and liberates Hofmeister into sanity. Lohman is the one sane person capable of deciphering these mysteries – of understanding Mabuse's scribblings or the cryptic word on the window pane. He might be a hero from Nordic mythology, inviolable to bullets, graced by some supernatural power. Not without reason do we first meet him humming a theme from the 'Ride of the Valkyrie' and whimsically claiming that dead police inspectors are taken to heaven on horseback. Allusions to the Nibelung Saga and to Wagner's *Ring* weave through

The Testament. Baum's destructive inheritance from Mabuse reminds us of Kriemhild, driven inexorably to revenge the death of Siegfried; his blowing up of the chemical factory recalls the twilight of the Gods and the final car chase through the countryside, with horses rearing up and a back projection in negative so that white trees swirl against a black sky (as in Cocteau's *Orphée*), takes us back to the 'Ride of the Valkyrie'.

This mythologizing is much more satisfactory than the religious allegory in *Metropolis*. It reveals, rather than confuses, the moral implications of the story. Mabuse and Baum (after his downfall, that is) are as mediocre as were most of the Nazi leaders. On the stage of this cosmic drama, though, they are seen to represent the disturbing ambiguities of evil – an evil often synonymous with insanity. As long as they have power over men they seem to be great shadowy monsters; when vanquished, they shrink into jerky puppets. But how is their power diminished? In part by love – the love Lille feels for Kent. Still, though love may be a bridge between evil and good, the lovers are too insipid to act as the film's only positive. As before, the burden finally lies with Lohman. Lang's criticism of the Nazis was not, it appears, veiled enough; and Goebbels banned the film. This ban might not have taken place if Lohman had been a less forceful creation. Anyhow, Lang had made up his mind about National Socialism; and, on the evidence of *The Testament*, it is hardly surprising that shortly after the ban he should have separated from his wife (who had joined the Nazi Party) and left Germany, first for France, then for America.

Few directors have had so wide an influence as he has. The historical importance of his lighting innovations and his sense of set design and frame composition have all been acknowledged; but not, I think, the power of his visual ideas. Few other directors have been so influential; one can trace the effect of his ideas in the work of such adverse people as Cocteau and Hitchcock, Kubrick and Carol Reed (*The Third Man*),

Godard and Frankenheimer, Losey and Wajda. But the director on whom Lang's early period has had the most seminal effect is Jacques Rivette.

D*

Jacques Rivette

At first sight Jacques Rivette's *Paris Nous Appartient* (1958–60), his one feature film, seems remote in kind from Lang's earlier work. The world organization, with its putative master-mind, is very much off stage. No one knows exactly who or what it is, and no one can be sure whether they are working for or against it. People change their views, probe anxiously, improvise – hoping to escape its trap. But whatever they do, it manages to destroy them one by one. On this level, *Paris Nous Appartient* offers us a Kafkaesque reversal to the Langian power game; we see things from the point of view of the postulant at the gate of the castle, the victim. The perpetual grey light of Rivette's Paris stirs up those dim, half defined questions that may come to us at dawn. We wonder whether we are surrounded by the tentacles of some elusive octopus, or by the last gliding shadows of night.

This conflict, this doubt, these questions, appear to be nebulous and without centre. Even the action wavers democratically over six or so principal characters, two or three plots; students and painters, theatre folk and poets – eccentrics all – living off their latent, perhaps non-existent talents. None can be placed by his role in society. Some of them seem mad from a sense of failure and persecution. Some of them have the most tenuous connection with the action, and are used, probably, because they are exotic: vivid ghosts with one rambling story. Hotels are the most frequent location – those dismal catacombs in which people are isolated from each other, or come and go leaving no memories. Travellers suddenly depart, rooms are found empty; the hope of security is continually undermined.

Communication is difficult to the point of being impossible. Neighbours speak some unfamiliar tongue. Life is provisional: café meals and canned food provide sustenance. There is no Lohman to whistle open doors or make connections.

We are jolted, possibly alarmed, by the contingency of events. Juan, a Spanish émigré, dies violently, and his friends don't know whether he has committed suicide or was murdered. The most they can be sure of is that before dying he composed and put on tape some 'apocalyptic' music, and that this tape has been stolen. Further suicides/murders happen, again without apparent motive. To a student caught up in the maelstrom, Anne Goupil, everybody seems to be playing the highest stakes in some unexplained game. Yet this high drama carries an undertow of immense weariness, the authentic dusty weariness of urban living. Anne's search for the missing tape, or the stage production in which she becomes involved, levy a toll quite incommensurate to their value; but then, there seems to be no way here of establishing a set of values. We are reminded of the disproportion between motive and action in 'M', and of Alain Resnais's *Muriel*, which also has no apparent centre. We feel like some eavesdropper listening to talk at the next café table – whispers about a plot to blow up the world. We, too, are drawn into the maelstrom . . .

Public events take place beside these private ones, but it is difficult to see how they relate to each other. The time is 1957, and there is mention of the OAS, the Falange, and of economic pressure groups. But we never learn whether any of these are *the* organization, and it doesn't appear likely they are. Nor do we see at once how the public and private worlds relate to the film's symbolism: its Biblical imagery – the Apocalypse, the Blood of the Lamb, Babylon – its play with such metaphysical ideas as that one man's death can bring about the end of the world, and that some people have the temporary power to become angelic guardians or ministers of death. Rivette changes focus with a Blakean disregard for the neat mind.

Such a disregard worked against the film on its first showing in London. Critics, reflecting on the way in which a sense of menace and an apparent formal incoherence encroach more and more on the film's drifting action, were inclined to dismiss it as a paranoid fantasy, uncontrolled and self-indulgent. Nevertheless, *Paris Nous Appartient* does have a form. 'If then I know myself only through myself,' wrote Coleridge in his *Biographia Literaria*, 'it is contradictory to require any other predicate of self but that of self-consciousness. Only in the self-consciousness of a spirit is there the required identity of object and representation; for herein consists the essence of a spirit, that it is self-representative.'

Such circumspection, so typical of a great deal of modern art, characterizes *Paris Nous Appartient*: its form lies in its attempt to be its own subject. Rivette creates this form through three of his characters, each of whose behaviour offers in turn a commentary on the action. One of these characters is Philip Kaufman, an American novelist claiming to be a victim of the McCarthy witch-hunts, who papers his room with drawings of savage mouths. Kaufman acts as a parody of the film's supposed paranoia, and in doing so sets the fantasy in context. He asks: 'Am I going mad, or is it the whole world?' The question is never resolved; but the self-reflexiveness of Rivette's world, with all its attendant ironies and ambiguities, hardly allows such a question to be resolved. It is a world bounded by enigmas, of which suicide, the act allowing of no afterthoughts, is the most impenetrable. 'There are some secrets men can't bear,' says Kaufman. But men *do* have to bear these secrets – the random actions of others, the absurdity of existence, the blankness of death. And Kaufman is the first person to lead Anne towards these mysteries. 'Those who think they are the masters are puppets,' he tells her. 'The real masters rule in secret and speak in riddles.' Kaufman lives up to his aphorisms. He seems to accrete violence and persecution – the sudden car accident, the swift betrayal. Is he a paranoiac or sybil, or, better, a paranoid sybil? We never are sure. After the catastrophe Terry,

111

a beautiful femme fatale, censures Anne for having taken Kaufman too seriously. The hostile organization, she claims, was entirely the product of his disordered mind – 'All nightmares are alibis,' she claims. And she blames the girl for the catastrophe: 'It's all your fault. You wanted the sublime.'

Yet Cassandra, too, was denigrated. Whatever Terry may say about Kaufman, her argument makes no sense of the meaningless deaths or of her own previous behaviour. A photograph of Antonin Artaud hangs in Kaufman's room. Artaud preached that life was dangerous, and that the arts should reflect this danger – the effect of a play or film should be as though a plague had broken out in the auditorium. He was considered insane and put away in a madhouse; still, gagging Artaud didn't make life less dangerous.

Gérard, a theatre producer trying to stage *Pericles* under desperate conditions, presents the second critique, in the sense that he stands for Rivette himself: his efforts to put on the play mime Rivette's difficulties in making the film – two years of money troubles and casting problems. You can trace one actor's career in other films by his having a beard in one scene and not in another; yet we so participate in the actual business of creating *Paris Nous Appartient* that this discrepancy doesn't strike us as incongruous. Life and art echo each other ironically; directors like Godard, Chabrol, Demy appear as actors – and Godard, the possible genius, comments on Gérard: 'He doesn't look like a genius. Like Modigliani he puts his genius into life.' Maybe this is no more than New Wave jokiness. However, Gérard's comments on *Pericles* are more serious, and tell us a great deal about the film's aesthetic. As he claims, on one level the structure of *Pericles* is loose and incomplete, on another ('from a global point of view') it holds together. 'A chaotic world,' he says, 'and yet like ours not absurd.'

Moreover, he believes his use of Juan's improvised guitar music will bring out the play's inherent unity in production. This music, we are told, is 'apocalyptic'; in other words, the

112

play coheres on a metaphysical level. The same applies to *Paris Nous Appartient*. 'I may seem normal,' says Gérard, 'but I feel as lost as though I were on Tierra del Fuego.' In the light of sudden death – above all, in the glare of mass death by nuclear weapons – the random existence of these apparently eccentric characters becomes significant. They, rather than the socially secure person, are seen to be closest to the human norm; since they, in spite of their neuroses, alone approach to some form of sanity. In such a way, the global viewpoint justifies Rivette's lyricism, whose resonance depends on its images being detached and unmotivated; confronted by the apocalypse, the world splits into fragments. The manner is similar to T. S. Eliot's *Gerontion* –

> '. . . Madame de Tornquist, in the dark room
> Shifting the candles; Fraülein von Kulp
> Who turned in the hall, one hand on the door . . .'

Extreme romanticism may prove disagreeable and extreme radicalism frightening; still, Rivette shows us the value of these positions by forcing us to live through them imaginatively – by making us aware of how necessary they are to at least one coherent interpretation of the world in an age of nuclear threat. At times the allegory may seem wilful, as in the case of Terry, the Cocteauesque angel of death, who protects Gérard until he takes on professional commitments and then abandons him to destruction. (There are overtones of Dr Mabuse in the weary way in which she carries out this duty as though it were a ritual.) At other times, the allegory takes on urgency, above all in the encounters between Anne and Juan's girls.

Anne, in fact, provides the third commentary on the action. Her search for the missing tape, a contemporary grail, acts as a critique of the film's theme – the search for its own form. Like Marina in *Pericles* she may be the innocent in the brothel-like city, but she is also the protagonist ('It's all your fault. You wanted the sublime'.) *Paris Nous Appartient* is a contemporary film, if only because it reverses the sexual hierarchy of myths; its women are the dynamic forces, healers and destroyers, while its men are ineffectual. For Rivette women are closer to the processes of life than men; and this may be why Anne's meeting with Juan's wife (who had a child by another man) and with Tanya Fedin (whom Juan, like some fumbling bee, promised a child without fulfilling his promise) are so vivid. Tanya, 'the last descendant of Genghis Khan', wears a board on her back like the flagellants, and provides the most brilliant description of the Apocalypse. 'The time is coming . . .' She tells of a man who died in London, and of how 'the stigmata of Hiroshima' was found on his body. Life is poisoned at its source; children drink the milk of death. She explains why the eccentrics must die – they live off the pulse, they *feel* the terrible mess man has made of the world – and in the language of Aldermaston she talks of their communality of purpose, 'our friends are our reflection', and of the world's attempt to suppress their message, 'we die because we are life'. In cold print Tanya's remarks sound pretentious, but in the context of Rivette's vision they ring true. *Paris Nous Appartient* is a testament of the New Left; it brings together certain attitudes that arose in the mid- and late fifties.

The mysterious organization defines itself within these terms. Against the spontaneous, the creative and the generous stands the calculating authority of the Establishment. Its creations are on the side of death: bombs, soulless cities – and it desires to wreck whatever may be new and exploratory. When it takes an extreme form, this authority goes Fascist (i.e. the OAS, the Falange). Rivette's anarchism is more self conscious, more cerebral than Vigo's, and so, in spite of its Millenarian colouring, less plausible; it remains a theory. Anarchism is a fuddled and hopeless attempt to abrogate the laws of politics. The beliefs of such anarchists as Vigo's father only make sense when we view them as an emotional force – when we remember how many of the anarchists were half crazy from starvation and oppression, and were in no state to think logically. In this day and age, then, Rivette's anarchism seems a little affected.

Lacking feeling, it lacks the intensity to make the organization appear a real power; it relies too much on concomitant evils to make its point – the cruel moralities of the French Resistance, of Algeria, and even of New Grub Street.

The representatives of this authority are usually grotesques. Its foremost agent in this film is the economist, de Georges, described as 'a walking anachronism' – a Spaniard and a compulsive neurotic, who plays finically with a telephone receiver, and who keeps a prim mad ballerina for a mistress ('my niece'), a twitching doll compared to the other women. But the boundary between the inchoate domain of the creative and the Establishment is easily crossed. Anne's brother, Pierre – 'a realist' – goes to work for de Georges and is estranged from her ('What's wrong,' he snarls as she tells him of her investigation, 'are you going mystical?'); in time he is murdered. Gérard also compromises and allows his production to be taken over by a professional management – and is driven to suicide. He, too, betrays Anne by relegating her part as Marina to a star actress.

The organization is most succinctly 'placed' in a sequence from *Metropolis* shown at a party: the building of the Tower of Babel – the sequence in which a race of slaves is forced into a vast and meaningless effort, eventually disrupted by the confusion of tongues. Rivette's choice of quotation is an example of how he is indebted to two of Lang's major themes: the city as an image of society, and the nature of communication. 'Paris belongs to us,' proclaims the film's title – and, indeed, the enveloping beauty of the city does make a home for the artist. The dawn of the Apocalypse is an hour of reassurance as well of reckoning; the chips are down. But the film's sombre epigraph is taken from Péguy – *Paris n'appartient à personne*. The dead city grows rapidly, like a cancer, and is quite uncontrollable.

Gabriel Pearson (in a broadcast) has well described the film's argument at this point. 'Cities are the supreme artifact. Here there is no nature. We are all builders of cities; and so we are all trapped in the cities other men build for us. Every city is Jerusalem or Babylon. Jerusalem is the ideal city of art and communication. Babylon is the city of destruction.' Such artifice requires its own unnatural morality – 'if Paris belongs to us, then we are responsible for its lives and deaths. Every death becomes a murder committed by us. We are responsible for our own deaths. Thus every murder is suicide and *vice versa*.'

A development of Spenglerian themes, perhaps, but Rivette's treatment of them is different from Lang's. The scenes of chaos and panic in 'M' and the *Dr Mabuse* series are handled omnipotently; we are not involved and we are liable to see them as comedy. In *Paris Nous Appartient* we are forced to undergo the perplexities of non-communication, the agony of living in a city where telephones are perpetually engaged and letters arrive too late. We, also, endure the endless prevarication of Anne's witnesses. In his moment of apparent triumph Gérard looks down from the rooftops and believes he possesses the city; but, unknowingly to him, it is as alien as Babylon. Though the world may in part embody our desires and ambitions, its totality remains ungraspable.

This distinction runs right through the film in the form of a deliberate split between plot and image; so that our impression is similar to one of being drunk at a party when, though the talk may baffle, we see people as though for the first time. Somehow Rivette's images take on this unusual lucidity, a lucidity which cuts across the turbulence of the action and is serene, almost oriental in its poise. Forced to see the world anew we discover a fresh disenchanted beauty in the expression on faces, on such mundane objects as telephones, lamps and books. This is the world as seen at dawn – mysterious, antediluvian and cold. Significantly, the final image of the film is of an unattainable and enigmatic loveliness, of Yeatsian swans treading lightly over water.

To be responsible is to accept and endure the unresolvable contradictions of the world, and to go on from there. After the catastrophe Anne, alone, asks, 'What shall we do now?' The stage manager answers, 'We shall restage *Pericles*'.

Federico Fellini

'If I were to make a film about the life of a sole,' said Federico Fellini, 'it would end up by being about me . . .' One would like to call his bluff; but one sees what he means. No other director has an ego so inflated, no other director's work is so directly autobiographical. The *oeuvre* is like a poet's diary, continually in search of something, immensely consistent in its development of themes.

The nature of this search is made clear in '8½' (1963). Guido Anselmi, the film director, is depressed and confined to a spa; he is unable to work on his latest project, and he is surrounded by a group of seemingly hostile figures. But fortunately his surroundings evoke memories of the past – he is haunted by suggestions of some half-forgotten beauty – and his companions cannot trouble him too deeply. When his scriptwriter objects to the scenario of his coming film, Guido has the presence of mind to realize that his kind of film cannot be created through the dictates of theory. 'Do you support the Catholics or the Communists?' asks the critic. But of course the question is far too simple. Like a man trapped in a car (as in his dream), Guido must try to free himself, especially from mere doctrine. His art, he realizes, must include all his past obsessions, all that makes up his present self. The irrational must enter so that the web of false symbolism, of false meanings, may be destroyed and the true candid images emerge. 'Are all lies and truth the same to you?' cries his wife. To which Guido might answer that lies and evasions are part of his search for the authentic self.

And so, though Fellini/Anselmi fears his critics – and in fantasy imagines them as driving him to suicide – he does finally manage to reject their taunts and exhortations. 'I am what I am and not what I want to be . . .' Much as Proust was unable to explain why the *petite madeleine* brought him such ecstasy (and took an unconscionable time in doing so), Fellini/Anselmi likewise is unable to discover why his images bring him such happiness. A magician summons up those inexplicably fascinating, personal images of people he can only love when they become part of himself, and these people join him in the glittering circus of childhood memory. Only then, as the circle is completed, can Fellini/Anselmi see how these images shore him against his ruin, and save him and his boyhood self – a child who plays the piccolo against the encroaching darkness.

Fellini likes greatly to use Roman Catholic ritual to suit his own ends; and '8½', perhaps purposely, takes the form of a confession. In this Fellini reminds us of another lapsed Roman Catholic. 'Wilde,' writes W. H. Auden, 'is the classic case of a man who wants to be loved for himself alone . . . Nothing is clearer in the history of the three trials than his unconscious desire that the truth should come out.' Fellini also assumes that to know all is to forgive all; there is nothing like a good confession for washing our dirty linen whiter than white. What is so cavalier about such magic – as used in a work of art anyway – is that Fellini/Anselmi expects us to condone everything. He tries to give the impression that he is the only real, lovable human being; because of which he feels free, like Madame Ranevsky, to let everyone down. Fellini/Anselmi in short is unable to make the distinction between the truths of the mind, in which lies and evasions are part of the totality, and the clearly knowable truths of behaviour.

It would be unfair, though, to doubt the courage of Fellini's confession. Quite justly his persona in '8½' feels persecuted by the critics. Most critics have been grudging in their praise of Fellini, and quite a number of them – those at any rate who are Marxist nannies – have taken great pleasure in giving him a regular thwacking. 'Out of this charivari of cruelty and gloom, of subtle malice and sentimentality, of introspection and half-baked mysticism,' said one of them, 'emerges a persistent note of squalor.'

The Italian tongue lends itself to superb invective, and Fellini's critics haven't spared themselves in exploiting this bias. But why are they so antagonistic towards him? Could it be that the world doesn't love a self-lover? In part maybe; but the truth of the matter, I would say, is that these critics see Fellini as 'a traitor to neo-realism'.

It is hard to see on what grounds they can so describe him. Neo-realism was more a state of mind than a worked out theory; 'a sense of expectation' said Fellini, and that is as good a definition as any. In 1943 Umberto Barbaro, a professor at the Centro Sperimentale Film School in Rome, made a highly rhetorical attack on Fascist rhetoric. He wanted, he claimed, a new kind of film that would rid itself of 'those grotesque fabrications which exclude human problems and the human point of view'. Neo-realism was to be an attempt to show things *as they were*, and not as the religious or secular authorities wanted them to be. The call was liberal, and it was a call to individual responsibility. 'The reality buried underneath myths slowly reflowered. Here was a tree; here a house; here a man eating, a man sleeping, a man crying,' wrote Cesare Zavattini.

Zavattini realized, one assumes, that this urge to escape artifice was as old as art – and that in the cinema it goes back as far as Lumière's brief sequence of a train steaming into a station. The exuberance with which the Italian film-makers surveyed, as though for the first time, the cold, wet, luminous world of the postwar years was new, however. There was a sense of re-birth; like the prisoners in *Fidelio*, these directors had come up into the light: partisans sink noiselessly beneath the bland waters of the Po, a father watches his hungry son devour a plate of spaghetti . . . 'What de Sica can do, I can't do,' boomed Orson Welles. 'I ran his *Shoeshine* over recently and the camera disappeared, the screen disappeared; it was just life . . .'

But alas life, pure life, when found unadulterated in a work of art becomes something of a bore; and neo-realism, though its originators didn't seem to realize it, was no more than that dullest form of art, naturalism. 'The first concern of the naturalistic writer,' said Zola, 'will be to collect his material and to find out what he can about the world he wants to describe . . . When all the material has been gathered, the novel will take place of its own accord.'

'Of its own accord' – with this simple phrase Zola manages to slip round the central problem of form. Such a legerdemain applies also to the neo-realists. None of them ever approached Zavattini's ideal of filming ninety consecutive minutes in a man's life; artistically speaking the project was far from feasible. They merely poured new insights into old forms: *Bicycle Thieves*, for instance, has the form of a well made play, while *La Terra Trema* (1948) has the form of a socialist realist novel. Moreover, though de Sica and Zavattini made humanist claims, they regress into child-cult and into an Augustinian despair at man's inability to solve his own problems. Visconti also lapses – in his case into the dialectic of history. The authority of Fascism gives way to the authority of the Vatican and the Kremlin. If anyone was treacherous, it was these directors surely. They lacked the technique – and possibly the will – to confront, as individuals, the problems of the post-war world.

Rossellini, who was probably the most liberal of these directors, shares their failure. In *Roma, Città Aperta* (1945) 'everything,' asserts Franco Valorba, 'was raised to an abstract ideal of liberty versus tyranny. But liberty from what and for what? And tyranny from what and for what?' Not only is the German intention left unexplored but, more seriously, 'both priest and communist use the same concepts of liberty, patriotism, and justice; each of them uses these concepts in a different way, yet each of them is unaware of the difference.'

Neo-realism was based on the assumption that I-am-a-camera, and that the camera never lies – well, not so long as *I* handle it.

124

This epistemological naïveté is endearing and somehow suits the excitement of the new age. But it could not last. There was a financial crisis; bliss faded as the dawn gave way to the complexities of day. The neo-realists fumbled, and some of the old guard were unable to cope with the challenge. Those who did however had to learn that the eye is more than a camera, and that our perceptions involve the need for discrimination; only then was the movement able to flower for a second, and perhaps more magnificent time.

Because of this, Fellini's search for the authentic self through fantasy takes on a historical significance. It may be no more than a coincidence that he directed his first feature in 1952, the year of the financial and ideological crisis; but I doubt it. If there had been no Fellini, we would have had to invent him. All the same, Fellini's interest for us doesn't lie alone in his concern for the inner world of fantasy which becomes tedious when divorced from ordinary happenings; nor does it lie in his ability to 'analyse sentiments'; Antonioni was already doing that in 1950, with *Cronaca di un Amore*, and with considerably more precision.

Antonioni and Fellini: a little like Tolstoy and Dostoevsky, Henry James and Dickens, they represent those polarities of experience which often seem to arise when an art form is at its peak. Ardent admirers of one are seldom ardent admirers of both. One remembers the bickering over *L'Avventura* and *La Dolce Vita* (both made in 1959): Antonioni was 'the more mature' said some, Fellini was 'the more exuberant' said others. Certainly Fellini cannot match Antonioni's insight into the sex-war. He is too much in love with himself for his lovers (well, for his women anyway) to be more than stereotypes. There is something sick about his idea of love too, which is completely sexless. The recurring situation in an Antonioni film is of a man trying to resolve a love-battle by what Wyndham Lewis calls 'amorous treatment, vigorously administered'; with Fellini, however, we have the eunuch, be it clown or half-wit, at the centre of the scene. This anti-eroticism disinfects everything.

Sexual disorder was the central theme in *La Dolce Vita* – and although the eunuch has an assured place in tragedy ('an achieved calm'), his role in such a study should have been peripheral, to say the least. The result was bizarre; one felt that Aunt Edna was working out the blueprint for an orgy in Highgate.

Fellini is very much an intuitive director, improvising on the floor, making up his mind at the last moment. ('To trap fleeting reality, one must avoid any suspicion of cold technique.') This spontaneity, egotism, and clearly neurotic reluctance to handle adult themes tempts one to try and describe his work in clinical terms. But such an approach would fail to tell us much, if anything, about the *quality* of his intelligence – his talent, if you will – and it is this singular quality which gives his films their importance and justifies our interest in them.

We are in the presence of an archaic mind which is, perhaps, unconscious of its singularity. Like a long-legged fly upon the stream, this mind moves over landscape and seashore, town and city, attuned to local texture and mood, remarkably sensible to each difference. Localities stimulate it more than anything else, yet the stimulus is more than one of atmosphere: many of these localities arouse an awe and a sense of communion which are best described as mystical. In *La Strada* (1954), Gelsomina, the half-crazed travelling player, communes with trees and telegraph poles; the world is sacred to her though she doesn't understand why. She meets an acrobat who is as blessed as herself, an angelic fool with whom she falls in love; and during their one moment of confrontation he tells her, echoing Hamlet, that everything in the world, even the smallest pebble, has a meaning. Shortly before her death Gelsomina is found clinging to a pebble as though it were an emblem of her faith.

Fellini has a feeling for the genius of a place – for those gods and demons who inhabit a specific locality. These gods are older and wilder than the Christian God; they are pagan gods, often nameless, often the dark gods celebrated by D. H. Lawrence.

126

But unlike Lawrence, Fellini never uses these gods as a major theme; it is as though he lacked the courage of his intuition. In *La Dolce Vita* a wild woman, possibly a medium, says that 'Italy is a land full of ancient cults.' She is one of a crowd of spectators waiting in a field for two children to carry out a faith-healing performance – the children claim to have had a vision of the Virgin Mary on this spot. But rain falls; the spectators flee, and the sick and lame are drenched. For Fellini the genius of a place can be illusive, can fail us, can sometimes be no more than a conceit.

Yet everything – his visual brilliance, his flair for atmosphere and mood – stems from locality. The castle at Bassano di Sutri, shrouded by night, with its Roman busts and its hollow stone rooms, is the scene for a cult of the dead. A party is in progress. Aristocrats, some of them slumbering, some of them dancing as though drugged, rise up like totems – enchanted, burdened by some abstracted despair for which their ancestors alone know the reason. A great door wheels open, and we see round a table princelings and sycophants gathered in the eerie rituals of a seance, seeking from the past some understanding of the present. At the end of a hall is a whispering well; voices carry from room to room a disembodied, false declaration of love. A masque of death: at dawn the guests proceed across a lawn and up a Palladian staircase, the women's gowns as elaborate as those worn at the court of Henri VI. Then the dead awaken: the family priest appears at the end of the garden, and the noble family, as though drawn by a thread, follow him to celebrate mass. Ruefully the other guests depart.

Some localities occur and obsess; one feels that Fellini has often journeyed through them, if not physically, at least in mind. If we were to draw a map of these localities we would find that they make a consistent world of the imagination. We would find, too, that this world has one broad division: between the provinces and the city.

Fellini was brought up in Rimini, and the provinces of his

imagination have the bleakness of the Adriatic coast. (Though one should add, perhaps, that his most complete study of provincial life, *I Vitelloni* (1953), was filmed at Viareggio, probably to release his powers of invention.) These provinces sub-divide into various regions, the most primitive of which is a rocky mountainside, studded with desolate crofts. Peasants, as flinty as their surroundings, inhabit these crofts; they are remote, dehumanized and speak an alien tongue; yet they are not without kindness. Zampanò, the Caliban of *La Strada*, perpetually returns to this mountainside, as though it were the one place he might call home.

Fellini appears to associate this place with memories of earliest childhood; the ages of man become a microcosm of the world's history, and we are here at the beginning of creation. The ASA NISI MASA sequence in '8½' gave us the most complete picture of this place: a primeval crone, her head concealed in a balaclava, sleeps in a high chair; sustained chords of music in a minor key shift and change; and there is a terrible sense of loss and desolation. Playing children are the one sign of life, yet their games are no more than glimpsed at, and remain as enigmatic as their laughter. The whole region presents us with a mystery; here the gangster Augusto in *Il Bidone* (1955) is left to die beside a mountain path and dying is redeemed as he sees peasants toil up this path; here, too, Gelsomina finds redemption. Yet the climate has nothing exotic about it; the air is fresh, clumps of snow melt between the rocks, and from a nearby monastery a bell sounds clearly. Many of the regions Fellini describes are familiar to us; none is so unusual as this mountainside with its aura of mystery and its deep sense of peace; none so extends our sensibility.

A similar mystery, perhaps a more theatrical one, bathes the provincial town at night: newspapers swirl round the piazza and lights sway in turbulent alleys. In *I Vitelloni* especially, where the five layabouts represent (we assume) various aspects of the youthful Fellini – though some of them are aged close on thirty – the provincial town is viewed through the eyes of adolescents. At night there is promise of exciting encounters or of pick-ups at cinemas. But at dawn, after the carnival, this promise turns out to be deceptive: the thought of love turns bitter when Alberto's sister runs away with a crook; ambition sinks back into torpor. By light of day the provincial town shows itself as oppressive.

Yet the town is not without gods, and these are often admirable. Fellini idealizes the provincial father, showing him as an honest, straightforward, *good* man who worships the gods of morality. But such a life is too dour for the layabouts; they crave for an easy life, for gods more exotic and more central to their needs. Bored, they stand on a jetty and contemplate the sea.

This seascape is familiar to us; it recurs more than any other Fellini locality – and it is the one locality that cries out for a symbolic interpretation. In this case it represents both the inner turbulence of the *vitelloni* – it spews up strange fish – and also, more importantly, it represents reality itself; all that baffles the understanding and chills the imagination.

The layabouts want to escape; yet at the film's end only one of them does so, the sensitive ingenuous Moraldo. As the train pulls out of the station, an elegant series of travelling shots shows us his friends asleep in bed. Perhaps these friends are sensible in not trying to realize their dreams; for though Moraldo may throw off the torpor of provincial life, his awakening will lead to disillusionment. The sequel to *I Vitelloni* was to have been *Moraldo in Città*, in which Moraldo was supposed to have fallen amongst con-men and tricksters. In time this sequel became the less dramatic but no less disillusioned *La Dolce Vita*.

The city, of course, is Rome; and the warring gods of this city preoccupy Fellini more than any other. Who are they, these gods? In '8½' Fellini/Anselmi asks a cardinal how he can find happiness, and is answered by a quotation from the eunuch Origen – only through the church can truth be found. He is then offered an uncompromising choice: *civitas dei* or *civitas diaboli*. We cut at once to a fashionable street and to the glamour of Cianciano. Guido has chosen damnation; but rightly so, perhaps, for he does find a temporary happiness in his images, in his dream of an innocent girl – a girl called, almost inevitably, Cardinale.

'For Freud, as for everyone else in the world, Rome means two things,' wrote Ernest Jones in his biography. 'There is ancient Rome whose culture gave birth to European civilization. Then there is Christian Rome that destroyed and supplanted the older one. This could only be an enemy to him . . . but then an enemy always comes between oneself and the loved object.'

For Fellini also, Rome is a double city whose allegiances cannot be reconciled. If we exclude the mediocre *Luci di Varietà*, which he co-directed with Alberto Lattuada, we find this conflict plays a major part in his first feature, *Lo Sciecco Bianco – The White Sheikh* (1952). Two provincials, Oscar and Wanda Cavalli, come to Rome on a honeymoon, on the last day of which they hope to attend a Papal audience. Wanda is a secret reader of *fumetti*, those Italian serials told in photographs, and is infatuated with the hero of one of these serials, The White Sheikh. Very much wanting to meet her idol, she slips off to the *fumetti* office on her first morning in Rome. By chance she passes a staircase down which actors in costume are descending. She is enchanted – to her the actors appear to be fabulous Bedouins and houris – and when some of them invite her to join them on a trip to the seaside where they are shooting the latest episode, she willingly agrees. And there, by the pitiless sea, she meets her White Sheikh and is disillisioned – the Sheikh turns out to be a philanderer. The girl runs away from the troupe and eventually returns to her husband. In the final scene she and her husband are reconciled, and hand in hand wend their way, not out of Eden, but across St Peter's Square and towards the Pope, beneath the benediction of stone angels.

This final scene, though moving, is unsatisfactory. The couple may be reconciled, but their reconciliation is childlike and seems an unlikely basis for a happy marriage. Nor can one believe that

Fellini wants the Pope to win over the White Sheikh – the enemy has come between him and the loved object. He is uneasy; he too is attracted by an apparently indefensible glamour. And because he is unable to defend this impulse he is forced to take refuge with the stone angels and the morality of the provincial fathers. His uneasiness shows itself in malice: he ridicules the Bersaglieri as they trot past in all their finery, and he exposes almost self-destructively the shabbiness of the *fumetti* actors. One critic (John Coleman) has justly claimed that Fellini is obsessed with the mediocre and the second-rate. Taking this one step further one could say that Fellini needs to destroy the metropolitan, and to turn it into the provincial; if he cannot belong to the glamorous city, then he must rob it of its glamour.

Though *civitas diaboli* may win out in his later films, Fellini continues to be troubled by it. Many people saw *La Dolce Vita* as a paean to the pleasures of an orgy, and ignored the irony of its title. Certainly there were 'pornographic moments', as regular as those in an Olympia Press novel and just as often fluffed, but the *tone* of the film was one of condemnation; one was reminded of the William Hickey column with its hypocritical prudery. The astounding success of *La Dolce Vita* can be put down, I think, to this effete dallying with *civitas diaboli*. Much of the action was incredible, yet many people swallowed it whole. One wonders why. Could it be that urban man has begun to accept the values of the popular press as a norm? Could it be that its eroticism and violence, its glitter and spangles, have become for him a kind of Nature?

However, Fellini's passion for unusual faces and for first-night crowds has another dimension. In '8½' someone says that 'it all stems from Scott Fitzgerald'. But even this is only true in part. Fitzgerald was attracted by the golden dream – by 'the extraordinary gift for hope, the romantic readiness' that lay beneath the dusty exterior of the Jazz Age. Fellini's obsession with glamour is far more primitive than Fitzgerald's, and is close to the *grammer* of witchcraft.

The 'smart' people and the film stars who make Roman society have the power of pagan gods; when the prostitute Cabiria is picked up by her favourite star she is unable to touch him. Indeed these people *are* pagan gods. When some of them first appear they are seen in mid-air, like icons of Christ in ascension: the White Sheikh is on a swing, Gelsomina's acrobat is on a tightrope, and the legendary Anita Ekberg descends from an aeroplane like a *diva ex machina*. Anita, of course, is Aphrodite or Venus, and quite the best thing in *La Dolce Vita*; she transforms *civitas dei* into her own kingdom as she paddles in the Fontana dei Trevi or walks down alleys with a kitten on her head. Through her the conflict between the two aspects of the city takes on visual complexity. Dressed as a cardinal she climbs to the top of the trembling dome of St Peter's and is goddess of all she surveys until her cardinal's hat is blown away – and rising up before the camera, blots out the city. *Civitas dei* remains omnipotent, though its inner sanctuary may be penetrated.

This omnipotence is rapidly diminished in 'The Temptation of Dr Antonio', Fellini's episode in *Boccaccio '70* (1962). Here Anita is without doubt a goddess whose glamour is witchcraft. She appears as a thirty-foot advertisement for milk, posted before the window of the prim and pious doctor. He is shocked by this exhibitionism and throws ink at the giantess. Enraged, she comes to life and teases him into submission by wreathing him in tulle and by dangling him over her capacious bosom. *Civitas diaboli* wins the day; but as one might infer from this grotesque situation, the victory is hardly one to be gloated over.

Does Fellini describe *civitas dei*, or is its presence merely felt by absence? One example suggests an answer. Fellini, we know, likes to secularize church ritual, especially processions. In *La Strada* Gelsomina watches four happy clowns dance along by a ditch playing fantastic musical instruments (similar figures appear at the end of '8½'). By contrast, we cut to a religious procession: trumpets bray, the crowd bows before holy images,

132

and the earth trembles. Our sense of *terribilità* is only diminished a little by the brief shot of a pig, crucified in a butcher's window.

The reason for this fear and disrespect of the Church is given in '8½' where the priests are shown as tormenting the child Anselmi into impotence. This is a fairly weak argument, and no doubt Fellini is being unjust to the Church. Still, no one would ever claim that Fellini's view of things was a balanced one. His is a religious mind, alienated from any particular religion, unable to conceive of a liberal, secular city (cf. his one agnostic intellectual, introduced by the characteristic line, 'Thanks to Father Franz I've at last found an ancient Sanskrit grammar. I've been trying to buy one everywhere'.) All the same, we would be wrong to think there was only one choice: between the terror of the Church and the hell of the *beau monde*; though this primitivism – fulfilled in the baroque style, the vividly etched images, the thunder and lightning – is powerful certainly, and reminds us of Wajda. (It reminds us too of Verdi, on whom Fellini, with his absurd anachronistic hat, appears to have modelled himself.)

Nonetheless, Fellini would probably agree with St Augustine that *civitas dei* is not to be found in the Church alone, if at all. In so far as it does manifest itself on earth, *civitas dei* is to be found in the lives of holy innocents – holy because they are in touch with the gods of the ancient Italian countryside. Some of them are religious; monks and nuns living in isolated communities, even the awesome cardinal who reads legends into a bird's song. Some of them are innocents in spite of themselves: the 'Umbrian angel', the station master's boy. But unfortunately this concept of innocence doesn't bear much close attention. We cannot believe in Gelsomina's madness nor in Cabiria's purity; we are conscious merely of the actress trying to sustain both character and symbol, and failing in both.

'When pastoral fails,' William Empson wrote, 'it takes refuge in child-cult.' The neo-realists often fail in this way. The de Sica–Zavattini combine, for instance, uses child-cult to escape from dealing with social problems on an adult level. The same is true

133

of Fellini. If we understand by innocence an idealized state of mind where guilt and anxiety have no place, then we must see Fellini's dream of innocence as escapist. Too often he tries to flee from the pressure of experience, nowhere more obviously than at the end of *La Dolce Vita*, where he retreats into a mawkish symbolism. Still, one has difficulty in dismissing this scene – as one has difficulty in dismissing anything of Fellini's. Though the characters may appear as false, the locality in which they breathe is so deeply realized that it takes on the clarity of vision – as figures move like dryads between the pine trees or wave to each other before a mysterious prospect of the sea.

Alain Resnais

No Trespassing reads the notice. The camera pans gently upwards and menacing chords of music fade into each other; a wire mesh slides past us, then dissolves into a gate of metal quatre-foil. Mist, and through the mist the dim outlines of a fabulous castle, as though painted on a backdrop. Close to us, the dark silhouettes of monkeys; then gondolas; then rococo gardens, always fading before the image of the castle . . . A courtyard, a mullion window, snow swirling, lips move.

This opening is taken, not from any film of Alain Resnais's, but from Welles's *Citizen Kane* (1941). One could think other-wise – understandably, since both men have a great deal in common besides their brilliance as film editors. *Citizen Kane* begins as though the film were still in embryo, taking shape in Welles's mind, in the hinterlands of thought. As images fuse or become defined, we are made aware, coldly, of the processes of creation. The actual and the dream-like are merged into a style giving them equal value. This reality doesn't break down into the subjective and the objective. Like Resnais, Welles relies on time and memory as devices to construct his plot. Kane is conjured up for us by the anecdotes of people who knew him; but each of these observers adds his own bias to their observa-tions. In the last resort, Welles would like us to believe that a complete definition of Kane is elusive. We may know the *how* but we fail to know the *why*; the man remains a mystery. Or so Welles would like us to believe. In fact, the jigsaw puzzle is complete. The omniscient camera shows us more than Kane's associates were able to know. The investigation into the man's life may be called off as a failure; but we at least are allowed to

137

see the burning toboggan, we at least know what 'Rosebud' was.

With Resnais, and especially with *I.'Année Dernière à Marienbad* (1961), the mystery remains an open one. From whose viewpoint do we see the action? From Resnais's, or from one of his characters? The question is slightly misleading, since the film is too impersonal to allow such viewpoints as the uncontrollable obsession or the random anecdote. Experiences are analysed and put together again with a scientist's dispassion. The result is a delicately adjusted artifact, which we are encouraged to describe principally in terms of style. Some critics harp on the belief that Resnais is troubled by problems of time and memory; but no sense of such anguish, of a man teased by a problem, disturbs the elegant surfaces of his work. Time and memory are tricks, ways of proliferating further doubts. Are the events taking place in the real world or in the minds of the characters? Did the supposed lovers really meet in Marienbad last year? We shall never know. We shall never know, that is, if Resnais undermines our confidence by juggling about with time and memory – which is exactly what he does. We are reminded of the watchmaker God: the spectator may suffer metaphysical anguish, not so their creator.

Welles and Resnais are as ecstatic in their detachment as Pythagoreans. Not for them the messy re-enactment of an already muddled human condition. Scrupulously, methodically, they discover rhythms and analogies, and form their structures. But they are as much interested in the processes of making objects as in the thing made: the memories, the dreams, 'the stray suggestion, the wandering word, the vague echo, at touch of which the imagination winces as at the pinch of some sharp point' – the Jamesian seed, in short, and its burgeoning. However, such a concern with the half-defined and the mysterious doesn't encourage them to be vague. Standing to one side, they continue to observe, precisely, sharply, much as a marine biologist might study the dark balletic sway of an octopus.

'In Xanadu did Kubla Khan/A stately pleasure dome decree...'
Welles plants this quotation heavily in the newsreel at the opening of his film; he is determined we should savour its point.
Kane's Xanadu is a repository for dreams, a phantasmagoria,
an egoist's burial ground. Here fragments of diverse cultures are
wilfully jammed into a grotesque, botched coherence. Here is
the last product of an over-reaching and fretful imagination.
The dreams clash, and their tarnished dissonance is like a nightmare – vulgar, opulent, and self-abnegating. (A terrible premonition of Welles's later career.) The full irony of the contrast
with Coleridge's pleasure dome is revealed.

This pleasure dome is, possibly, a symbol of the perfect work
of art. It rises above caverns measureless to man, through
which runs the sacred river, Alph. This river, we remember,
sprang from a deep romantic chasm, a place as holy and enchanted as ever was haunted 'by a woman wailing for her demon
lover'. After passing through the caverns it sinks in tumult to
a lifeless sea. According to this reading, then, art begins in
feeling, but may refine itself into lifelessness. Such an excessive
refinement is sometimes ascribed to Resnais. According to this
view, his pleasure domes are built too far down river from the
deep romantic chasm; they lack vitality and feeling.

Is this so? A test case would be to ask whether, in fact, his
women do wail for demon lovers. In a sense they do. Each of
his three feature films deals with the sexual awakening of a
woman: the actress in *Hiroshima Mon Amour* (1959) is
released from an emotional block by her Japanese lover,
admittedly a rather genteel demon; the woman A in *Marienbad*
is aroused and possibly abducted by the man X (insipid in
Giorgio Albertazzi's performance); while Hélène Aughain in
Muriel is also disturbed by the return of her ex-lover, the
confidence trickster Alphonse. So women and demons of a sort
are in evidence; more suspect, in truth, is the nature of their
wailing. Resnais's understanding of the effects of love is unusual,
to say the least. His women may be stirred into desire, but in

no case does this change lead to a new warmth, to an opening up of the world's possibilities, to hopes of a shared future with the lover. Instead, it leads to a morbid withdrawal into self, into speculations about the elusive nature of the past and about the baffling uncertainty of the present. Are these women's feelings really supposed to be unfrozen; or is Resnais so frozen himself that he is incapable of showing them as otherwise? One of his favourite films is Visconti's *White Nights* (based on Dostoevsky's novel), in which a young man encounters an ideal girl in the atmospheric nights of a seaport, and then loses her to another man. The two lovers have no contact – don't, if I remember rightly, even touch each other. Their meeting might have taken place in the young man's mind.

Resnais's films, also, might be no more than convolute dreams. The most extreme of them, *Marienbad*, is totally self-reflexive – and to this extent, recalls *Paris Nous Appartient*. Indeed, both films show us people trying to shake themselves free from a shared and increasingly possessive incubus. But there is one important difference between them. Resnais never shows this escape to have happened. He deliberately sacrifices the actual world to style – to the setting of the action in a mythical place, to numerous and obvious exclusions. (His characters, for instance, have no proper names and often act without apparent motive.) *Paris Nous Appartient* in part works on the level of such a style; but the contingency of its action, the multiplicity of its characters and plots, and especially the fact of its taking place in present-day Paris breaks the fantasy and allows the viscous, slippery and opaque world to creep through.

Resnais doesn't appear much interested in cities as places representing the human condition. In retrospect, the Hiroshima and Nevers of *Hiroshima Mon Amour* seem empty, windblown places where the self-sufficient heroine is free to luxuriate in tantrums. The silent tracking shots through these cities seal us off from urban noise and distraction; we might be concealed behind glass. The Boulogne of *Muriel* is more realized, yet it fails to exist in its own right. For the most part, like the jumble in her flat, it reflects the disorder in Hélène's mind – as when unrealistically, superbly, a liner rides up onto the promenade.

The city is hardly relevant, doesn't even function as a context. Resnais and his characters don't seem aware of their withdrawal from common life. Again, compare Kane's Xanadu with the hotel in *Marienbad*. To my mind *Citizen Kane* is one of the few good films made in the socialist realist tradition – a portrait of capitalist society from a Marxist viewpoint. The young Kane is an idealist, who wishes to fight for the rights of the under-privileged; as much a 'citizen' as any French revolutionary. In later life he tells his crotchety guardian, almost a travesty of the capitalist banker, 'I would like to have been all that you hate most'. But Kane's idealism is destroyed by his wilfulness which, as Welles makes clear, is fed by the intoxicating power of a private income and of a society whose values are based on greed. The withdrawal into Xanadu is no more than the final repetition of such a wilfulness; Kane's life there is as much an awe-inspiring mess as his activities in the outside world. Resnais, on the other hand, doesn't even hint at the possibility of such a failure. His starting point is the fabulous, enclosed private world. The hotel in *Marienbad*, like Welles's Xanadu, reminds us of Kafka's castle insofar as an apparent Authority resides there ('the best people'), yet this is an authority confused, dying, cut off from general experience.

Richard Roud has claimed* that Resnais with his friends Agnès Varda and Chris Marker 'have inherited the legacy of the thirties: a passionate concern about politics and social problems and a conviction that these problems have a place in the realm of art', and he contrasts them with those pure cineastes, Godard and Truffaut, whom (he thinks) feel that the cinema's 'essence is in its rawness, its direct communication of experience – like Hitchcock, like Hawks'. I don't really sense this contrast myself; nor would I go to Hitchcock and Hawks for the 'direct communication of experience'. Besides, if Resnais is aware of the

* *Sight and Sound* (Winter 1962–3).

political and social problems of our time, he sees them – as far as his films are concerned – from within his pleasure dome. His documentary, *Guernica* (1950), makes use of some of Picasso's pictures, ranging from the pink and blue period to those associated with Guernica, to comment on the Spanish Civil War; it is as much about Picasso's range of style as an actual event. The Guernica paintings are, above all else, attempts to express the horror of war. (Though as far as I'm concerned, the feeling behind them doesn't match up to the claims of their rhetoric.) But Resnais refuses to honour this intention; he deliberately alienates us from feeling. The self-conscious montage, especially in the light bulb sequence, the carefully written poem-commentary by Paul Éluard read by Maria Casarès with an exemplary diction, continue to remind us that we are *not* watching a transparency through which the world can be seen, but a film-object, an artifact engraved with the rhythms of high tragedy.

Resnais likes to parade his virtuosity. He has gathered about him some of the best film technicians in France, such as Henri Colpi and Jasmine Chasney (editors) and Sacha Vierny (cameraman). He appears to rejoice in the belief that he and his team can make beautiful objects out of anything: a novelettish script by Marguerite Duras, newsreels of the concentration camps, an experimental piece of writing by Alain Robbe-Grillet, a documentary about plastics. The actual world is no more than pap to feed a style.

Nevertheless, though Resnais can be over-demonstrative in his mastery of technique, his films are not cerebral, as is such a comparable exercise in style as Roger Leenhardt's *Rendezvous at Midnight*. In spite of their coldness, they compel us and draw on our emotions; while those of his imitators seldom do. It is difficult to pin down why. A similar problem faces us in the case of Antonioni – his ability to animate scenes and shots that in the work of lesser talents would seem protracted. Antonioni brings off such a *tour de force*, I believe, by the sheer intensity of his nervous energy. For instance, almost every shot of *The*

Eclipse is vivid with a sense of endured discovery. Antonioni, I feel, is probing into the unknown; even though he may lapse into the absurd, as he sometimes does in *The Red Desert*, he nearly always conveys an explorer's tension. Resnais holds us by other means. On the evidence of his work, I would say that he was a rationalist fascinated by the nature of art, by qualities in art that the pure rationalist hesitates to find in himself – sensibility, imagination, feeling. Resnais's detachment, then, is but one side of an internal conflict. The pure rationalist may feel divorced from the mysterious creative processes working within him, yet he is also baffled, even amazed by them. If he is honest, he seeks to come to terms with them, as though searching for a lost part of himself. Resnais's trek through this half-known landscape is like a compulsion succumbed to reluctantly; its conflicts underlie all his work.

Welles's detachment is of a different kind. He doesn't take a story and film it straightforwardly. As Penelope Houston has said, his method in both *Citizen Kane* and *The Magnificent Ambersons* is to comment wittily on a banal story – one that is implied rather than stated. The story, in fact, is jettisoned and the wit remains. Kane's attempt to build up his second wife, Susan Alexander, into a great prima donna is handled with callous verve. She may be tiresome, dull and an appalling singer; and yet, without intending to, Kane makes her suffer to the point of destroying her. Perhaps rightly, Welles underplays the pathos of the situation; it would have needed a Judy Garland to make it interesting. He stresses, rather, the backstage excitement of Susan's first night in the opera, *Salammbo*: the plump women in the chorus running hither and thither, the agitated maestro bellowing last-minute instructions, the solemn music as the curtain rises and the darkness of the auditorium emerges from beyond the footlights. Susan and her misery are ignored; we are merely given a shot of her pretty legs as she steps forward. Then the camera climbs up and up, in one of the most dazzling shots in the cinema, past ropes and flats to a couple of stagehands listening to her first notes from the top catwalk. One of them puts two fingers to his nose.

The flamboyance and mannerisms of grand opera are appropriate to the styles of both these directors; yet when Resnais treats the salon play in *Marienbad* with a comparable verve, the result is shrouded in menace and closer to Racine than to Welles. In *Cinema Eye, Cinema Ear*, John Russell Taylor mentions the constant references to *Citizen Kane* in Resnais's short about the Bibliothèque Nationale, *Toute la Mémoire du Monde* (1956) – one example being, he writes, 'the camera roaming casually over a litter of boxes and cases which recall precisely the same treatment of the packing cases in Xanadu'. Granted: but Welles's Xanadu appears as a carefree place when compared to Resnais's vision of the Bibliothèque. The packing cases of Xanadu are never more than mere packing cases containing loot – the bizarre legacy of a recent Tamburlaine. But Resnais makes the dusty piles of books and manuscripts of the Bibliothèque seem fearful objects; in the half-light of this enclosed building where the outside world doesn't exist they appear to be as self-generating as a brain tumour. (*'Ma pensée se pense'*). And the liquid tracking shots, the enclosed spirals, the criss-crossing of attendants add to our claustrophobia. If Resnais is indebted to anyone at this point it would be to Georges Franju – the Franju of *Hôtel des Invalides* (1952) – with his inexplicable talent for making the oppressive and the dissonant seem beautiful. In the field of painting, Francis Bacon has a similar effect; but then, in the case of all these artists we are not far from the origins of Romanticism, of Medusa's head. We had thought ourselves to be outside the aquarium in *Toute la Mémoire du Monde*; but, unsuspectingly, those tracking shots have drawn us in – and we are slowly drawn towards the half-awakened octopus . . . Resnais's Bibliothèque has too many dark corners for my comfort.

Yet once again . . . I walk on, once again, down these corridors, through these halls, these galleries, in this structure . . . from another century, this enormous, luxurious, baroque . . . lugubrious hotel . . . Again, tracking shots of rich ceilings, chandeliers and glistening ornamentation. Again, we are drawn into the Mallarmean world of mirror reflections (*'Je m'apparus en toi comme une ombre lointaine'*). The symbolist atmosphere of *Marienbad* is very much Resnais's own contribution to the film, and little of it is to be found in Alain Robbe-Grillet's script.

Robbe-Grillet, despite his avant-garde trappings, is, I believe, a naturalistic writer whose naturalism is merely taken to an extreme. His third novel, *La Jalousie*, demonstrates this most plainly. The narrator – a cuckold in a commonplace love triangle – never comments on the action. He records the world as if he were, quite literally, the passive eye of a camera. When he describes his wife in her day-to-day life he uses the same terms as when he describes her photograph. The distinction between an event and a photograph of an event is broken down. Life is reduced to a series of photographs; and Robbe-Grillet's listing of such an inventory parodies the naturalistic accumulation of things. The relationship of husband, wife and lover is evoked through these photographs – by the way in which they are presented without any sort of chronology. Sometimes a photograph is repeated, sometimes we return to an earlier one, sometimes we leap forward to one which, in time, is quite out of order. As these same flat descriptions recur in artful confusion, we recognize them as emblems for the disorder of a mind sick with jealousy.

But, in at least one way, Robbe-Grillet's heroes are non-naturalistic. Like the symbolist poets they live in isolation, and are forced to dream out some nightmarish vision in order to fulfil themselves. Yet the reason for this obsession is obscure. *La Jalousie* is not primarily about jealousy, nor *Le Voyeur* about a man troubled by the thought that he might have committed rape. The motive in each case is the need for revelation. And such a motive holds true for *Marienbad*. Robbe-Grillet has said that the film is 'the story of a conviction: it has to do with the reality the hero creates out of his own words and

145

vision'. The man X, trying to break out of his narcissistic isolation into the actual world, is no more than one of those phantoms beloved of by the Romantics.

But Robbe-Grillet's script only becomes truly symbolist in Resnais's treatment. For example, in the script the statue in the garden is merely a piece of stone into which the characters read their fantasies, much as we might read all sorts of memories into a faded snapshot. In the film, a superb play between camera-work and sound transforms this statue into an image, so that like the symbolist image of the dancer, it embodies life-in-death and death-in-life to the point that it almost speaks.

Robbe-Grillet has claimed that we can interpret the film in any way we wish to. In other words, the film is like the imagery in a symbolist poem, to the extent that it refuses to disclose itself to Cartesian explanations; we need to apprehend it sensuously as we would, say, a piece of music. As one might expect, this type of action opens up a wide range of ambiguities – since in the light of reason the imagination appears to be a labyrinth where certitude doesn't exist, only possibility. In *Marienbad* you can never say 'this is so' about anything, only 'it might be so'. One cannot say of an image that it is true or false, merely that it is possible. Of these images, the principle ones are associated with various zones in the hotel and the adjoining gardens. They embody a number of alternatives. The bedroom of the woman A is a place where love, murder or rape might take place – together, singly, or not at all! Part of the garden represents the possible meeting of the man X and the woman A during the previous year. The salons, where the recurring matchstick games are played, is the zone where X perhaps challenges his double, M, the man 'who might be A's husband'. The most important of these images, however, is the total one of the hotel and its surrounding estates. This image is not equivocal, since it represents an absolute – the ideal of the imagination, Xanadu itself, the perfect work of art.

In *Marienbad* Resnais has created 'an artifice of eternity'. As a rationalist he has tried to test the faculty of imagination by pushing it to an extreme. In effect, he has revived the *fin de siècle* cult of Byzantium:

> A starlit or a moonlit dome disdains
> All that man is,
> All mere complexities,
> The fury and the mire of human veins.

In practice, *Marienbad* only partially creates this artifice. The bejewelled guests grouped stiffly around card-tables and staircases are too modish to evoke the chilled self-sufficiency of the Byzantine emperors, of Justinian and of Theodora, as we see them in the great mosaics of Constantinople and Ravenna. Images of the supernatural, their eyes stare beyond us into the unknown. Not so the guests in *Marienbad*, who merely give the impression of being frozen and ill at ease. 'Decor is everything in these works,' wrote Mario Praz of the nineteenth-century Byzantine cult. 'But the meticulous catalogues of trappings, of objects, of acts, don't merely aim at giving an atmosphere. The ferment of impure, violent deeds which these decors have witnessed, underlies the description of them.'

Resnais provides us with the meticulous catalogues, but he doesn't quite convince us of the impure violent deeds. The broken tumbler, the woman A lying dishevelled on her bed, appear more as embarrassing accidents than as intimations of some barely suppressed horror. And the guests' formality is more an attempt to conceal petulance at being caught in an eternal recurrence, rather than dark cruelty. Only at times, as in the final image of the hotel at night, its silhouette reflected in water, does the film visually fulfil its intention.

But all the same, Resnais does succeed in giving us a sense of court life.

'It must always be remembered that our greatest authors have nearly always written about the court,' claimed Valéry.

'They drew on the life of the city only for comedy, and the country for fables. But the greatest art – the art of integrated forms and pure types of characters, entities which permit the symmetrical, and so to speak the musical development of a quite isolated situation – is bound up with the existence of a society governed by convention, where a language is spoken that is adorned with veils and furnished with limits, where *to seem* controls *to be,* and holds it nobly in constraint, which changes the whole of life into an exercise in the control of the mind.'

Sometimes they order things a little too well in France. Still, this authoritarian view of the 'greatest art' does cast a pale glow on *Marienbad.* Resnais is fascinated by courtesy, by polished surfaces beneath which the power impulse operates. *To seem* controls *to be* (What exactly are the motives of the two men?), while the sustained rhythm of images, the beautiful convolutions of dialogue, provide a 'musical development of an isolated situation'. The plot itself is close to court tales. X claims to have waited a year for the woman A, to give her time to choose whether she will elope with him or stay with the man M. This motif of 'a year and a day' recurs in fairy stories; yet it also plays a part in that most realistic of court novels, *The Princess of Cleves.* Even the match games are reminiscent of jousts . . .

Like Agnès Varda who made a documentary about a group of models at work in castles on the Loire, *Ô Saisons, Ô Chateaux* (*1956*), (and very much unlike his other close friend, Chris Marker), Resnais is haunted by such past glories as the court of Louis XIV – a vision appropriate to the epoch of Mon Général. The two lovers in *Hiroshima Mon Amour* are so like court ambassadors that you can't be sure whether they are supposed to be people in their own right or purely representatives of Hiroshima and Nevers: they respond to each other with touchy correctness, and exchange glances with a diplomatic caution. And their complicated sexual manoeuvres at the opening of the film are as formal as the signing of a treaty, though Pauline Kael* was tempted to see them as some kind of perversion – 'it irresistibly set off lewd speculation about just *what* was going on. And what was the stuff they were covered with? Beach sand? Gold dust? Ashes? Finally, I accepted it as symbolic bomb-ash, but wasn't happy with it'.

In *Hiroshima Mon Amour* the court analogy is applied laxly; it might have strayed in by chance, as though Resnais were unable to shake off his dream of the past and of court virtues. But he was able to use this dream more effectively, to contrast it with a present-day grim truth, in his picture of the concentration camps, *Night and Fog* (1955). The caste system of the camps was as inviolable as those of any court: the prisoners, the kapos, the SS ('the untouchables'), and the Commandant who, says the commentary, 'presided over the rites from afar and pretended to be unaware of the camp. But he was aware . . .' *To seem* controls *to be* – or almost. The scriptwriter, Jean Cayrol, flays at this incongruity. 'A concentration camp is built like a stadium or a grand hotel with *entrepreneurs*, specifications, an open market for contracts and, no doubt, bottles of wine. No fixed style . . . The imagination is free to choose the alpine style, the garage style, the Japanese style, or no style at all.' The crudely applied patina of civilization takes in nobody; rather, it heightens the pervasive sense of nightmare. On one side, the murders, tortures and degradations. On the other, a parody of civilized virtues so grotesque that it makes Welles's Xanadu seem mellow in comparison – the camp symphony orchestra, the zoo, the greenhouses where Himmler grew fragile plants, the so-called hospital and prison, even Goethe's oak around which Buchenwald was built. Yet travesty or no, tourists even now visit the camps as though on a jaunt to Versailles.

Resnais characteristically views this recent past from the present. It allows him to be cool, to bring out the ironies of madness. Germany had virtually lost the war, yet Himmler continued to supervise the blueprints for further gas chambers.

* Fantasies of the Art House Audience. *Sight and Sound*, Winter 1961–2.

Coal was needed for the war effort, yet priority was given to the supply for the camp furnaces. And as the Third Reich crumbled, trainloads of prisoners were lost or forgotten in sidings . . . Resnais wants to place this terrible farce within the context of reason; he doesn't seek to curdle our emotions. The music is by Brecht's favourite composer, Hans Eisler: a spare atonal score, mostly for solo flute. And like Brecht, Resnais wants to draw us back, to make us think.

The opening sequence, and all the scenes taking place in the present, are shot in Eastmancolor. Resnais dwells on the beauty of the camps now – dwells on day and sunlight. Crows rise from a cornfield. A tracking camera moves at an oblique angle to the camp so that we are not enclosed by it; we see the ruined buildings and the barbed wire as objects, as a kind of wild sculpture. We are here as witnesses, not prisoners.

Then we move into the past; and Resnais makes sure that we think of it as remote from now. There is none of the immediacy of drama, no re-creation by actors – merely stills and newsreel clips in monochrome, a dossier recollected in tranquillity. As Resnais shows, understatement and the direct approach are far more painful than the liquid darkness and implied perversions of Andrzej Munk's *Passenger* (1961). Robbed of their black magic, the camp experiences no longer strain the imagination. We can relate them to daily life; they become more real, and so more terrible. Resnais, I believe, has created an honourable work of art out of what I had once thought of as intractable material; and for me, anyway, *Night and Fog* justifies his stature as a major director.

Jean Cayrol is also the scriptwriter of *Muriel* (1963). Here Resnais again surveys some irrational threat to the pure rationalist's position. Now, instead of being concerned with the mysterious processes of creation, the logic of images, the rituals of camps or the madness of war he turns to a subject which the pure rationalist finds just as threatening – the realm of pure feeling. At first sight, *Muriel* reminds me of those weird George

Kelly plays – do they exist? – which Mary McCarthy claims to have seen. She describes them as *not* being polite comedies, 'though well made and set in drawing rooms' – and 'though performed by actors, their heroes and heroines are glasses of water, pocketbooks, telephones and after-dinner coffee cups'. The personalities of the Kelly women are, she says, 'fluctuating and discontinuous. Emotions with these characters is a kind of bird mimicry of emotion. Like amateur actors they can't hold the pattern'.

Hélène Aughain could be one of these women. Brought up in Boulogne, she lost her bearings when the city was blitzed, and now lives a hand-to-mouth existence. She gambles compulsively on borrowed money and sells antiques from her flat which she has turned into a shop. Yet Hélène's flat appears to reflect a general disorder. Roland de Smoke, her splendidly named best friend, owns a junkyard and tries to keep up appearances in a wilderness of bedsteads. The new Boulogne of jerry-built flats rests uneasily on an old landscape. A liner misses the harbour and, lights blazing, rides up on to the promenade.

On one level, *Muriel* is like a parody of the 'well made' play. It opens on a predictable situation: Hélène summons up the past in the form of a long unmet lover, Alphonse, who turns out to be, almost inevitably, as deceptive as memory itself – a confidence trickster, duping himself as much as others. Most of his pretensions are false; he never made films in Cairo, ran a night club in Algeria, nor was received at *le palais de Buckingham*. Hélène is forced to realize that her past was no more than *une histoire banale*, while Alphonse, worn down by Hélène's disorder, ages and loses something of his confidence. In the final act a *deus ex machina* turns up to unravel the plot – Alphonse's brother in law, a grocer named Ernest. As in many 'well made' plays, there is also a sub-plot that echoes the action of the main one. Hélène's step-son, Bernard, and his best friend, Robert, while serving as paratroopers in Algeria, tortured to death an unknown girl they named Muriel. Bernard tries to free himself from this past by murdering Robert.

But *Muriel's* resemblance to a 'well made' play becomes strained if we take it further. Henri Bernstein, a master of *la pièce bien-faite*, once said that the basic device in comedy is misunderstanding. In *Muriel* misunderstandings are piled on with such liberality that the device soon becomes a burlesque of itself. The characters seem intelligent and alert, yet nothing works out as they want it to. 'What happened to you on your birthday?' asked Alphonse of a meeting that should have taken place twenty years before. 'I waited for you at home,' answers Hélène, 'and had to eat cold prawns for two days.' 'And I,' he murmurs, 'was saddled with a packed luncheon basket.'

Muriel is as perplexing as a Chinese puzzle. Sequences lead up to recognitions that never take place; when recognitions *do* occur, they happen so unexpectedly as to leave the characters at a loss. On the evening when Alphonse returns to Hélène – bringing his mistress, Françoise, whom he introduces as his cousin – one expects a grand encounter; but instead Hélène goes off after dinner to gamble with Roland de Smoke. All through *Muriel* people keep popping up without warning, and then are abruptly dropped – just as one begins to think they might be important.

This disorder extends to beyond the action. *Muriel* gives the impression of being the work of an insane editor who has tagged together, quite haphazardly, all the bits and pieces of film usually left on the cutting room floor. When Hélène and Alphonse are having their first heart-to-heart, we cut back and forth from them to Roland de Smoke ascending in a lift, or to Bernard and Françoise as they dawdle outside bars. In the same way, Ernest's denouement is undermined by blank shots of a newly built block of flats.

Possibly the imagination can flourish in an ivory tower. But emotions have to operate in the world in order to exist; they need to have an object. According to Sartre (*Sketch for A Theory of the Emotions*), feelings arise when we can no longer reasonably cope with the world. 'When the paths before us become difficult,' he writes, 'or when we cannot see our way, we try to change the world; that is, we live in it as though the relations between things and their potentialities were not governed by deterministic processes but by magic.' In effect, this is what happens to the characters in *Muriel*. Continually their projects – their plans to control the future – are blocked by misunderstandings, so that they are forced to retreat into a world of emotion and magic. In turn, their emotions play havoc with their memory. 'When we're afraid,' says Hélène, 'we forget.' So each of the characters is forced to create a past and a future for themselves and for others which is only partially true.

In *Muriel* Resnais merges the actual and the dreamlike much as Welles did in the opening moments of *Citizen Kane*. The distinction between subjective and objective doesn't exist; we are shown people being driven into emotion. *Muriel* works on the level of the particular. When Hélène stumbles on a doorstep, we note it is one particular woman, one particular doorstep. Resnais's characters are caught up in a dense, opaque world which they cannot understand emotionally. They are snarled up by things: they live through their tape-recorders, diaries and cameras; bump about amongst antique furniture and junk; are enmeshed by problems of money. Above all, and naturally, they are preoccupied by problems of food. *Muriel* is a gastronomic orgy: people are always cooking, or discussing recipes, or stuffing themselves with goodies.

This materialism threatens to engulf them, and they try to save themselves by making dramatic gestures or platitudes about time and money. Much of the humour in *Muriel* arises out of this attempt to generalize about obdurate facts. Alphonse, standing behind Hélène, makes a declaration of love. She swings round, and he finds she is holding a cake beneath his nose.

But we, the audience, cannot feel superior to this bad faith. We, too, cling to the generalizations about time and memory,

153

hoping they will give us some clue to the film's meaning; we, too, are bewildered by its uncompromising stress on the particular. The originality of *Muriel*, I would say, lies in the attack it makes on the spectator's habitual sense of superiority.

Usually as spectators we feel we are in control of the film; we know the rules of the convention, and we know, more or less, where we are going. This aloofness allows us to view films rationally. We fail to see the world in its magical aspect, where anything might happen; we expect films to obey the rational laws of the 'well made' play. But in *Muriel* we are continually being thrown off balance and thrust back into the bewildering undergrowth of feelings. We might, for instance, believe that Hélène is its central character – that we are concerned with her interior dialogue. In fact, Hélène and her flat are no more than a meeting point, a juncture, for the other characters. Passers-by are just as important as she is. 'Can you tell me how to get to the centre of the town?' asks a man, briefly glimpsed. A woman answers, 'It's here . . .' The centre of *Muriel*, our focusing point, is both everywhere and nowhere; at one moment Hélène is at the centre of our attention, at another she is a stranger to us, a voice overheard in a bar.

We are never allowed to linger. Constantly we, the audience, are forced to realize our misunderstanding of what has happened; constantly we are forced to change our viewpoint. These shifts of consciousness remind us of the wide-ranging technique employed by Virginia Woolf in *Jacob's Room* and *Between the Acts*. But whereas Mrs Woolf's transitions can be brooded over and do relate to some central theme, Resnais's transitions are violent and abrupt, and act as a denial of all centrality.

And yet *Muriel* strikes us from the start as having a tightly controlled form. In its final moments, especially, as the various misunderstandings are dovetailed into each other – Hélène goes to the wrong railway station, while a woman (presumably

Alphonse's wife) wanders into Hélène's flat – we have a sense of reconciliation. We feel as though we had been listening to a finely organized piece of music. Indeed, I believe music is our key to understanding the form of *Muriel*. Hans Werner Henze's score for it is serialist; and the serialists, I think, have provided Resnais with his method. Like them he starts from a series of arbitrarily chosen laws which he then observes with an icy rigour.

To me, this experiment doesn't seem contrived. Resnais, I feel, has been able to find an impersonal order in the disordered feelings of his characters, and without faking the evidence; the subjective and the objective are fused into a style. This style is reminiscent of the opening to *Citizen Kane*, but technically much enriched. We could use it, perhaps, to gauge how far one aspect of the cinema has developed in twenty years.

Max Ophuls

It would be easy to think of Max Ophuls as a hedonist, as a creator of operettas – of champagne and roses, of artifice and elegance, of the refinements of passion. The time is usually turn of century, the architecture baroque; and we are well sealed off from the anguish and rough edges of the immediate present. Ophuls, so it seems, goes to extravagant lengths to preserve this bell-jar atmosphere. He shows a voluptuous concern for textures and pleasing compositions. We might permanently be watching some play in an over-heated theatre; the natural never breaks this web of illusion. Snow (when used, and it is often used) seldom looks cold and never turns to sludge. It usually seems to be stage snow – warm and fibrous, though gleaming. Cities are seen from a distance and hardly ever are the real thing. Often they are meticulously constructed models of late nineteenth-century cities – controllable, neatly shaped, no urban sprawl. The camera roams about and above them with impunity. We think of Schniztler and the never-ending girations of the carousel, of Lehar rather than Wagner. The mood doesn't eddy beyond the bitter-sweet; it is all there in the weary elegance of an Anton Walbrook.

But this impression, however vivid, is mostly false. In fact, Ophuls was no Viennese mourning the loss of the Austro-Hungarian empire. He came, rather, from the pre-eminently bourgeois district of Sarrebruck on the Rhine, and at the age of sixteen formed a society whose principal aim was to protest at the decadence of the times! He may have taken care in re-creating the period before his birth (he was born in 1902); but I doubt whether he ever identified himself with this past.

159

At all times Ophuls was a professional, a *regisseur* preoccupied with the niceties of style and with giving the public a visual feast. He was, above all, a man of the theatre, a creator of illusions.

In truth, he was circumscribed by illusions. Possibly he was unable to believe in the emotions associated with fulfilled love and thought them as no more than counterfeit; anyhow, in his work there is little mutual trust. His idea of pleasure is often a matter of keeping up appearances – of elderly men and their cocottes play-acting at happiness. Relationships are so frequently arranged on a cash basis, that perhaps he believed love only existed when it was unfulfilled, as in the *Letter from an Unknown Woman* (1948). Yet he was no Marxist. He didn't appear to think that a change in the social structure would bring about happiness. His revolutionaries are usually ardent bores. He was, if anything, a bourgeois moralist, and a rather savage one at that; the one point of contact between all the lovers in *La Ronde* (1950) is probably syphilis. And yet, though he may have been bourgeois, he doesn't extol bourgeois virtues. His Darbys and Joans are very dull indeed. No, his tone is less one of nostalgia than of frustration. To escape from boredom into unsanctioned pleasure is to court danger. The promise of happiness has to be paid for by a duel in the snow, a lingering death, or a public degradation. The gods of this morality are terribly harsh.

And so we should not allow Ophuls' taste for the baroque, for opulence, for pathos, to remind us of Erich von Stroheim. These two directors had little in common, in spite of the fact that they were both Jewish exiles whose allegiance was first and foremost to the public and who, as natural showmen, encouraged a false legend to build up around them. The dismal fate of Stroheim's heroines in *The Wedding March* (1927) and *Queen Kelly* (1928) is dwarfed by the imposing decor and alleviated by the director's easy cynicism. His world is above all solid and established; as in the theatre, intrigue can be enjoyed there for its own sake. Stroheim is a precursor of Billy Wilder rather than of Ophuls. For Ophuls is far less assured. There is something self-immolating about his talent. Claude Beylie has argued that his restless camerawork, his passion for tracking shots, continually eradicates the solidity of his decor, so that, in his later films especially, those sumptuous baroque sets, built with a scrupulous care for detail and often at a great cost, are passed over rapidly, casually, as though they were some insubstantial pageant. James Mason once quipped:

> 'A shot that does not call for tracks
> Is agony for poor dear Max,
> Who separated from his dolly,
> Is wrapped in deepest melancholy.'

Restlessness is like a nervous tic. Maybe his experiences as an exile had something to do with it; or, maybe, like Renoir, he wanted to free his actors from the tyranny of the held shot. But perhaps there was another, more permanent reason for this ceaseless movement – in that Ophuls saw life as a flux. He assumed, perhaps wrongly, that the more passionately a woman lives the more rapidly she burns herself out. At the heart of his vision is a void. Energy, by its nature, devours itself. Intentions are self-destroying. His son said of him: 'He was an extremely serious man – a moralist, troubled, even pessimistic. He once claimed that an *informed* pessimism, capable of being held in check, and so allowing one to enjoy life was the most adult way of looking at things.'

The one thing he believed in completely was the theatrical – the reflecting mirrors of illusion, the creation of style out of despair. Interestingly enough, he long wanted to make a film out of *Six Characters in Search of an Author*. The director closest to him in spirit is François Truffaut; above all, the Truffaut of *Jules and Jim* (1961). There again we have the *impression* of a golden world – an amiable Bohemia and a charming Bavaria. But, as in advertisements, this beauty is only skin deep. *Jules and Jim* ends with a spiteful madness – a suicide and a murder – and, finally, the blank wisdom of the crematorium. The tone may be light to the point of being flippant; and the

161

F

sun may continue to shine. Yet we can't help feeling that this happiness is only half of the story, and even then, possibly, a trick of the mind. True reality is to be found in the cold cruel world of the broken home or the reformatory to which we must always return; much as the boy in *Les Quatre Cents Coups* (1958) was only able to escape for a while into the dubious paradise of the Parisian streets. Truffaut may have realized his affinity to Ophuls, for the actor cast to play Jules, Oskar Werner, is also the student in Ophuls' *Lola Montès* (1955), and this subterranean sort of homage is typically New Wave. If so, Truffaut went rightly to *Lola Montès*; for though this film was mutilated by its distributors and had slight returns at the box office, it is now rightly seen (having been restored) as Ophuls' masterpiece. All his interests are there, both elaborated and fulfilled.

Ostensibly, the subject is the life of the great courtesan who was mistress, amongst others, to Franz Liszt and the King of Bavaria. But when we read about the real-life model for this subject we learn, surprisingly, how Ophuls has thrown away a considerable number of opportunities. Maria Dolores Eliza Regina Gilbert (1818–61) was a far more robust figure than he made out and lived a far more extravagant life – amongst other things she made a fortune and for a while ruled Bavaria single-handed. Ophuls' Lola is passive, as dull as a sex symbol that turns out to be more symbolic than sexual (perhaps the dullness of Martine Carol's performance was intended). The fact is that Ophuls was bored by this untalented, flamboyant dancer. As he once said, 'I don't have much liking for people who live overfull lives.' His Lola was merely a pretext, a peg on which to hang the reactions of the people around her.

This point becomes clear when we come to Ophuls' most striking emendation. At the end of her life Madame Gilbert was converted to Episcopalianism and, plump and comfortable, died in New York, a triumph to her profession. The exhausted and dying Lola Montès, on the contrary, is forced by poverty to join an American circus, where spectators are allowed to excoriate her with questions about her past life. This vast and fabulous circus has no basis in reality; yet it is the *raison d'être* of the film, the centre of the action from which the past is recalled in flashback. It provides Ophuls with the perfect device by which to dissect his heroine publically, and the reference to contemporary life is plain. 'At the time,' he once said, referring to the genesis of his plot, 'I was reading newspapers and I was struck by a series of news items which, directly or indirectly, took me back to Lola: Judy Garland's nervous breakdown, the sentimental adventures of Zsa Zsa Gabor. I meditated on the tragic brevity of careers today. The questions asked by the audience in *Lola* were inspired by certain radio programmes.' In fact, the form of these questions was shaped by certain questions Ophuls had asked in some anti-Nazi wartime broadcasts made for the Free French.

The circus embodies the modern world of mass publicity in all its cruel indifference – the modern world, in particular, of America and Hollywood. But *Lola Montès* isn't primarily an indictment of the American way of life. True, the ringmaster is like a Hollywood tycoon of the thirties. When he hires Lola he tells her that she can't sing or dance, but, like his piano-playing elephant, can provoke scandals and so is a worthwhile attraction. In turn, she says she always does as she likes, and he answers, 'That's what my elephant thought. But he learnt to play the piano. Now he adores music . . .' Yet this ringmaster, as played by Peter Ustinov, is very much the middle European impresario – mordant, sulky and excessively refined. And the circus, though presenting a Roman spectacle, is most exquisitely conceived. The new world may be distasteful in its methods but it is hardly worse than the old; perhaps in the last resort there is not much to choose between them.

In a sense, Lola's confession gives an unfair picture of the past. Any life would look tarnished when exposed to such a glare. But all the same, save for her short idyll with the King of Bavaria, this past (and so the old world itself) appears to have

163

been as miserable as the present. The critic of bourgeois society in Ophuls was unrelenting.

'At the heart of our profession,' he said, 'is the circus.' The circus is the one reality, the cold centre to his universe, the epitome of his style. The royal blue and gold credits fade, and from the darkness above smoking chandelier lamps are lowered softly. Then, to an oriental tinkling we become aware of rows upon rows of girls in scarlet uniforms juggling silver saucers. The Mammoth circus is like 'an antre as shadowy as night', and so vast that we can't see its enclosing tent. Here is the *reducto ad absurdum* of Ophuls' self-negating architecture: an all-containing structure that resembles a void. Like St Peter's in Rome it arouses a sense of vertigo; there is no point of focus, and we feel disorientated. This vista, both enclosing and unending, reminds me of Welles' Xanadu and Lang's Metropolis. We feel we could go on walking in it for ever and never reach the circumference, never escape.

Recent discoveries in the field of technology may have aggravated this modern feeling of endless power and ceaseless dissipation; but in art we can go back at least to the Mannerists to discover its first impression. Aldous Huxley has written of the *Carceri* etchings of Piranesi:

'The most disquieting fact about these dungeons is the pointlessness that reigns throughout. The architecture is colossal and magnificent. One is made to feel that the genius of great artists and the labour of innumerable slaves have gone into the creation of these movements, every detail of which is completely without purpose . . . Even where the enclosure is more or less complete, Piranesi always contrives to give the impression that this colossal pointlessness goes on indefinitely, and is co-extensive with the universe.'

The Mammoth circus is exactly like this – a bringing together, without purpose, of numerous details and sudden effects. There is continual movement, like the random shaking of a kaleidoscope. The ringmaster is standing before us square and solid in a multi-coloured suffusion of light; in the next shot he surprises us by shooting up through a trapdoor. All the Mannerist tricks are put to use. The camera is everywhere; in the centre of the ring at one moment, it swings round in a 360 degree arc, in contrary motion to a troupe of circling horses. Illusion is undermined by illusion. Some clowns run on; and it takes us a second to realize they are dwarfs. They are followed by more clowns – and again we are disturbed, for these clowns turn out to be giants.

The circus may represent Lola's mental purgatory, the consequence of her failure to discover a stable relationship. By the end of the performance the ring has become squalid. There is a cold blue light, and discarded cigarette packets and orange peel lie in the sand. Members of the audience are invited up to kiss Lola's hand, a dollar a time. The degradation is complete.

But just as importantly, the circus represents the dangerous swamps of art itself. We are absorbed completely into a world of the imagination, a world as exotic and complete as Cathay, a world of opalescent lights, of immediate effects and shuddering depths which bewilder us to such an extent that we are made vulnerable to the most outrageous symbolism. The owner of the circus, for instance, symbolizes death in all its forms; he wears a clown's make-up, smokes cigars, counts huge stacks of money and has a skull by his desk But we are *not* reminded of Ingmar Bergman. The atmosphere is too rich, too voluptuous, too bewildering, for us to be aware at once of the intellectual framework to these sequences. The treatment of this circus is, needless to say, remote from naturalism. The royal blues, plush reds and golds are reminiscent of Veronese and Manet, and make a fine contrast with the more sober colourings of the flashbacks. *Lola Montès* is one of the first films to use Cinemascope, and few since have used it with such majesty.

'At the heart of our profession is the circus . . .' Truth has no place in a world of total illusion, and will appear as false as everything else. The devices of biography are exposed in this arena, as well as Lola's character. The past is made threadbare by the luxurious props used to recall it. Clowns and acrobats in candy-white costumes and make-up act out Lola's youth. Later she, swaying perilously on a low tightrope, re-walks her travels from Rome to Budapest, then to Warsaw and to Moscow. (At each stage of the tightrope there is a precise model of these cities.) It is as though Christ, hired at some great fee, were to play Himself in a cycle of Mystery plays . . . Ophuls has often preferred sketches to feature-length stories (cf. *Le Plaisir* (1957), and *La Ronde*); but in this case he has found a satisfactory way in which to bring together his sketches. All the tricks and devices of compression and detached comment are brought to bear here as wittily as in *Citizen Kane;* we have the same sense of technical discovery of the cinema being tested to its limits. But, unlike Welles, Ophuls' cynicism is reluctant, and I would feel uneasy if I tried to identify him with the bland ringmaster who so selfconsciously *glows*, as though he were the one pearl in this oyster-bed.

And yet, as with the ringmaster, there is something crude at times about Ophuls' sensibility. The musical joke in *La Maison Tellier* of associating the theme of *Jesu, Joy of Man's Desiring* with a whores' outing goes a little too far; as, indeed, does the marshmallow taste in *Lola Montès* of dressing up a third class cabin on a steamer in velvet and silks. Ophuls had pretentions towards grandeur and liked to make a display. When Lola first meets the King of Bavaria in his apartments and deliberately tears her dress so as to stay with him, the King goes to the guard at the door and asks for a needle and thread. The order is passed down a hierarchy of servants and across halls and courtyards of the palace until the whole establishment is in an uproar. There is something amusingly childlike about this fuss, something reminiscent of the King in *When We Were Very Young*, asking for some butter for the Royal slice of bread. Peter Ustinov wrote in an obituary that Ophuls was like, 'a watchmaker intent on making the smallest watch in the world, and then, with a sudden flash of perversity, putting it up on a cathedral.' In *Lola Montès* this brilliant perversity took the form of building a colossal circus around the confessions of a courtesan.

Amidst all the swirl and *trompe l'oeil* is Lola, as impassive as a Buddha. In the earlier circus scenes she seldom moves; she rises on a throne through a trapdoor or attendants carry her about on a litter. Even her face is immobile. Her answers to the audience's questions are oracular and never really explain her life. As the ringmaster says, 'We try to discover our follies anew and our replies take the form of questions.' In a totally illusive world there can be no such thing as a 'true confession'; one can merely perpetuate further illusions. Lola is an enigma, and in this she is a cousin to the cool amoral heroines of Godard and Truffaut. But she is enigmatic because she has been reduced to an object, not because she has a secret to hide. 'All rights over her life are owned by the Mammoth circus,' says the ringmaster. 'Can't be reproduced elsewhere.' I am reminded of those Hollywood screen bosses who allegedly tried to subjugate stars like Garbo and Louise Brooks – and who, when the stars rebelled, damaged Garbo and ruined Brooks; and how, more subtlely, perhaps unconsciously, tried to dehumanize these stars on the screen by turning them into *things*, into sex-objects or goddesses.

But Lola's downfall also carried religious overtones. The similarity of Ophuls' camerawork to Dreyer's in *La Passion de Jeanne d'Arc* (1928) – the general baroque flow contrasted with static close-ups on Lola/Jeanne – may be no more than a coincidence. But her penitent's robes in the final sequence, or the possibility that the circus may be a place of purgation are less of a coincidence. Lola is like a prostitute in having to 'die' many times a day; but death and renewal are also true of a soul in purgatory. The tragic hero falls from a great height. Lola's tragedy is that, though at every performance she has to leap from a great height, she cannot die. In retrospect, this religious

167

element gives depth to the flashbacks – to Lola's restless pilgrimage from lover to lover. Each of these episodes takes us through a different season, from spring to winter, so that Lola becomes *una signora di tutte le stagioni*. But the circus remains, binding these episodes together; and the circus, we feel, is timeless. The aimless journey of Lola's coach, as it moves through cities and crosses plains is opposed to the unbreakable circle of the ring where the rider is forced to circle back into the same place. Like his heroine, Ophuls had known penury and exile; he, too, had been the eternal traveller forced to live off his wits, and forced to live for the moment only. ('Has the journey tired you?' asks a friend. 'No,' answers Lola, 'if the inn and the dinner are good it will pass.')

Yet I am reluctant to press the religious parallel too far. Ophuls was a dying man when he made this masterpiece, and *Lola*, perhaps unintentionally, reflects his exhaustion. The film makes no religious affirmation. Lola's travels are too random and haphazard, and the probings at the circus fail to give them meaning. Energy devours itself, and the greater the energy the more rapid the annihilation: here, surely, is Lola's destiny. If anywhere, the film's theme lies in a quotation read to her from *Hamlet* by the deaf and moribund King of Bavaria:

> 'How weary, stale, flat and unprofitable
> Seem to me all the uses of this world!'

Andrzej Wajda

'We were living at the bottom of a huge crater, and the sky far above was the only element we shared with the other people on the face of the earth. All this was in his verse – grayness, fog, gloom, and death. Still, his was not a poetry of grievance but of icy stoicism. The poems of this entire generation lacked faith. The fundamental motif was a call to arms and a vision of death. Unlike young poets of other epochs, they did not see death as a romantic theme but as a real presence.'

'Only a passion for truth could have saved him from developing into the person he became. Then, it is true, he would not have written the novel about the old communist and demoralised Polish youth. He had allowed himself the luxury of pity, but only once he was within a framework safe from the censors' reproaches. In his desire to win approbation he had simplified his picture to conform to the wishes of the Party. One compromise leads to a second and a third until at last, though everything one says may be perfectly logical, it no longer has anything in common with the flesh and blood of living people.'

CZESLAW MILOSZ – *The Captive Mind*
(The second extract refers presumably to Jerzy Andrzejewski, author of *Ashes and Diamonds*.)

There is a curious little scene at the opening of *Ivan the Terrible* (Part II) when Prince Kurbsky, one of the Tsar's oldest friends, betrays him and appears at the Polish court. This scene jars with the general style of the film; but such a jarring, I believe, was intended. I think that Eisenstein wanted to show the Polish court – where predators mask cunning beneath a foppish elegance, and light jests are exchanged about Russian barbarism

– as being shallow and effete when compared to the supposedly noble tyranny of Ivan's court.

As usual, Eisenstein caricatures his opponents. But for once, though, his caricature does bear some relation to the truth. Perhaps this Roundhead could understand the Cavalier point of view because he was himself something of a Cavalier by temperament. It is a truism that the Russians and the Poles are usually hostile to each other; and though the situation has reversed since the days of Ivan, and it is the Poles who are now under Russian pressure, the old tension remains – aggravated maybe by the fact that Poland is still under the aegis of Russia.

The style of Andrzej Wajda shows all the traces of such a tension. He may be a Marxist – by conviction or by necessity – and his early work may have made the expected obeisances to the Party, but he is also very much the Polish artist. Unwittingly or not, he allows the past to creep through into his work in the form of a typically Polish style. Like Prince Kurbsky, he cannot resist either the flamboyant elegance or the code of honour of the old Polish court.

This style has similarities to the Polish baroque art of the Counter Reformation. There is the same love of elaboration and of visual energy. All the same, Wajda is not, like Pasolini, a Marxist unable to resist his Catholic inheritance. Polish baroque art flourished when the Church went secular and assumed the powers of a court; and the court is the seminal influence on both this art and Wajda's style. It only makes sense when we see it in terms of courtliness, courtesy, and above all courtship. 'If you are agreed that a bunch of roses means love,' said Wajda in an interview,* 'a director will use it in a film just to mean that. But what Buñuel does, and what I try to do, is to create new images which could play the role of symbols. You surely know the saying, "The first man to compare a woman to a flower was a genius; the second was a fool".'

Young animals like Stach in *A Generation* (1954), Maciek in *Ashes and Diamonds* (1958), or the more cold-blooded Andrzej

* *Films and Filming*, November 1961.

in *Innocent Sorcerers* (1961) are all humanized by the rituals of courtship. The war forces Maciek especially into brutality. Yet when he falls in love he becomes as delicate and original as any of his ancestors. Never banal, he manages to speak about even his deepest feelings with wit. Wajda has a similar temperament. In his trilogy he engages passionately with the major themes of war. Yet because he is so serious a director, some critics have felt inclined to describe such baroque effects as the upturned creaking crucifix in *Ashes and Diamonds* as superfluous. They don't realize that elaboration is an essential part of Wajda's way of viewing things. Wajda the Marxist and Wajda the man of feeling don't preclude Wajda the courtier. On the contrary, the three are inseparable.

Inseparable, and yet antagonistic. The Marxist has little time for the courtier, yet is forced to accept his presence; and so, though the Marxist may scoff at the pre-war Poland of the Generals, he cannot suppress the courtier who is haunted by the past and defines himself by recalling it. Maciek wins the hotel porter's confidence by playing on his nostalgia for old Warsaw; he also lights vodka glasses to the memory of his dead friends. There is always ambivalence and irony. You can feel it in the scene when Szczuka, the tired Party secretary, plays Spanish civil war songs on, of all things, a gramophone with a huge horn. You can feel it in the presentation of the silly but likable count, ghost of the ancient regime, or most obviously in the discordant Polonaise at the end of the film that softens into a dream procession. Significantly, when Colonel Staniewicz, the anti-Communist resistance leader, goes to the phone there is a landscape painting behind him, so that he appears to be answering the phone in Arcadia. The past is like such a landscape, remote and a little foolish. Yet it is by such a past that the present is measured. It gives meaning to Wajda's brooding concern with the difference between generations. Moreover, though this past may be often grotesque, it does at least belong to Poland.

Most of Wajda's feelings about the past are captured in *Lotna* (1959), whose subject is the last stand of the Polish cavalry in the autumn of 1939. The film opens with the battalion watching a beautiful white mare, Lotna, stream across a field beneath a pure blue sky while shells explode about her. Presently two cavalry officers enter a luxurious yet empty chateau. From the floor above they hear the sound of hooves. They go upstairs, and discover a bedridden general. Beside the bed stands Lotna, whom the general bequeaths to the battalion. The officers accept her; as yet, they do not realize she will lead them all to their deaths.

But, as Wajda shows, Lotna is no symbol of death. Destruction, rather, is brought about by an attitude of mind – typical of which is the belief that a white mare can lead the cavalry into victory against German tanks. The cavalry is elegant, courteous – and sealed off from the contemporary world. Fleeing citizens push cars and carts up a muddy slope; in the background the aloof cavalry glide past. They have just passed by the time the Messerschmidts arrive to raze down the sweating citizens. Wajda acknowledged their crazy luck; he films lovingly their grace and beauty. But at the end Lotna lies quivering, with a broken leg caught in a gunwheel. Entrails hang steaming from trees. A field is turned into a butcher's shop.

The deliberate incongruities of *Lotna* are too cerebral to have a dream resonance. They are not Surrealist; they are more like the conceits of metaphysical poetry. Some of the comparisons may be bizarre, but the logic connecting them is usually rational. *Lotna* is crammed with fanciful comparisons: a spur catches on to some blood-red berries, a coffin is found full of ripe red apples, a wedding veil catches on this coffin's lid. But these bright ideas never take on dramatic life. Somehow it doesn't matter that the dead horses should look like models or their blood be so clearly paint, for they are no more than concepts in some brilliant theory which is stillborn, choked by its own cleverness.

In *Lotna* Wajda over-reaches himself; his talent for ingenious elaboration is unchecked. In other words, we find here those Polish qualities Eisenstein mocked at and probably envied. Yet Wajda can be cruel too, can turn the tables and do an Eisenstein, and look at the Russians just as disdainfully.

Otherwise, it is something of a mystery why he went to Nicolai Leskov's *The Lady Macbeth of the Mensk District* for a subject. Leskov's short story is a study in provincial boredom, of a woman who murders her father-in-law, husband and nephew so that she and her lover, Sergei, can live together undisturbed. The parallel with Shakespeare's play is misleading. Leskov's Katerina is ruthless and brave, and the local people nickname her Lady Macbeth; in every other sense, the structure and tone of the story is different from its source. It could be argued, in fact, that Leskov is trying to refute Shakespeare's idealism. In a far from ideal world heroic behaviour, be it good or bad, has no chance to sustain itself; the boring grey comedy of life soon wears it down. 'Ecstasies tire,' wrote Leskov, 'and the inevitable prose returns'. Katerina is destroyed by mere accident, and not by the consequences of her crimes; there is no talion justice, and her punishment appeases no guilt.

Wajda transforms this story, dramatizes it, makes it sharp with contrasts. The characters in his *Siberian Lady Macbeth* (1961) are as mannered as icons, and have a touch of *Ivan the Terrible* about them. Perhaps Wajda's interest in Russia is no more than an aesthetic one – the old Russia of priests and rituals and savage moujiks. Though he is fascinated by his panther-like heroine – who is brutal, yet haunted by the wish to have children – she doesn't provide him with anything new. Wajda marks time, plays about with the *texture* of Russian life. He is very much the tourist, amused, detached – the sophisticated Pole eyeing the barbarians – and the detachment works to the detriment of feeling. The murders which should be terrifying, tend to spill over into black comedy. The pressures of religion, so important to the action, aren't treated with enough insight. The material is well wrought to the point of being contrived; and the astute handling of Cinemascope is too selfconscious to be convincing.

Katerina's fate is a random one. Her passion collapses into futility. Here, possibly, was Wajda's stimulus, though the impulse gets lost in the resulting tour of the Russian scene. Leskov belonged to no party. He was a man of conscience, whose talent relied on observation rather than dogma. Inevitably, one of his contemporaries labelled him 'a secret, cunning and insinuating Nihilist.' In his wish not to compromise, or to fake up ideals, Leskov is like Katerina – and, I imagine, like Wajda. Certainly in the final sequence Wajda does convey the inherent bitterness of Leskov's story. Katerina and Sergei, condemned to penal servitude in Siberia, are marched across the Steppes with a gang of convicts. The wind howls and sheets of dust swirl across the bleak landscape. This is a hell similar to the one where Maciek died – a hell without purgation, a descent into total cynicism and despair. But Katerina is unbroken. Her lover takes another mistress, and in a gesture of defiance she drowns both this woman and herself. Her passion may have proved futile, yet she refuses to accept this fact. She believes it better to die than to deny her own being.

Yet how can she have *being* without the driving force of some conviction? How can passion, or the will to live, exist without ideals? Wajda's films continually raise such questions. The problem is to live without hope in an age of captivity, and yet not to retreat into an emotional numbness. This problem, I believe, challenges Wajda himself as much as his characters. In *Lotna* and the *Siberian Lady Macbeth* he dabbled with effects, he posed; but his earlier work was strikingly different. In those days Wajda did *appear* to have an ideology – almost excessively so. The Marxism of his first film, *A Generation*, is laid on with academic correctness. When Sekula, the foreman and Party member, explains to young Stach why he must resist the Germans, he talks of the class struggle and says reverently, and in close-up, 'a clever old man with a beard worked it out'.

He pauses, and before we can mutter God, continues, 'His name was Karl Marx'.

Sekula and Stach are stereotypes familiar to us from socialist realist literature, and *A Generation* has its full measure of tired political slogans. Still, it is a remarkable film if only because it takes on life in spite of these impositions. From the start Wajda's talent relies on observation and not dogma; he slyly refuses to toe the Party line. Later, as the brief thaw sets in, he is to express himself more freely. But, always, he puts himself forward as a representative of his generation, and not of the Party.

A Generation claims our attention as a searing personal document of what it was like to be an adolescent Pole at the time of the Resistance. Wajda's young men and women are confused and they blunder. They are forced under the stress of war to discover their own values, and these values are not those of the Party. Admittedly, Stach and his girl friend do all the right things – the bored meeting, the shared cigarette – and, in fact, Stach only becomes real to us after the Gestapo have carted off his girl. Yet fortunately he is not the emotional centre of the film; this centre, rather, is his companion and *alter ego*, Jasio.

Jasio is terrified by the thought of death – and this physical terror is the most immediate fact about him. *It is also the most immediate fact about Wajda's trilogy.* To die when one is drained by age may be a tolerable fate; but to die suddenly when one is throbbing with life is an inconceivable terror. Yet it is exactly such a terror that Wajda makes us face. *Kanal* (1957) is an appalling nightmare in which Resistance fighters are trapped in the Warsaw sewers with Germans waiting to shoot them at every man-hole. (An extended metaphor of terror which, I am told, Wajda has deliberately exaggerated. In reality, most of the arrested partisans were given a bottle of vodka and a blanket). At the end of *Ashes and Diamonds* Maciek must endure a stumbling protracted death in a field of rubbish; we are spared little of his agony.

This pattern of terror and annihilation is established in *A Generation*. The Germans have made reprisals, and their victims hang from lamp-posts by the Vistula. Jasio, passing, looks up. Almost unconsciously he touches his throat. The camera tracks past other onlookers, most of them old and impassive . . .

Jasio is tormented by a series of contradictions, many of them of his own making. He is an uncommitted man caught up in a war and unable to make decisions. He has no loyalty, no honour. When the Ghetto is burnt down and a Jewish friend comes to him for sanctuary, he is so afraid that he turns the friend away. At the same time, though terrified of death, he is overwhelmed by the pleasure of shooting a German soldier in a bistro. He vacillates always; refuses to join Stach's Resistance group, then offers to help when he senses Stach's disdain. (But how hollow Stach's right-mindedness appears in comparison!) On his first expedition with the group he fails. He is supposed to be acting as a sentry – and yet, as soon as he sees two German soldiers walking along idly, he panics, runs, and so attracts their fire. The panic turns out to be as unwarranted and fatal as the one that leads to Maciek's death. Suddenly the plot twists into a grotesque and fearful nightmare. Jasio clatters through a brewery, an art gallery, and past a man with dark glasses and a board of holy images. Shots echo about him. He climbs a spiral staircase, and the soldiers follow. He is irretrievably trapped. At the top of the stairs he comes to a shuttered window – his last hope of escape. He tugs open the shutters and finds the window barred. The Germans have almost reached him; his pistol is empty; he leaps from the stair balustrade and falls many floors to his death.

This sequence enacts rather than depicts a nightmare. We also must live its terror: are driven up the stairs, discover the barred window, face the choice of suicide or surrender. The experience doesn't call for common sense, and we are too inundated by it to view it logically. We don't consider the implausibility of the chase (why do the rifle shots always sound so close?); much as we don't question the implausible geography of the sewers in *Kanal*. Wajda conjures up a state of mind, not an actual event; and disorientation and distortion are the natural effects of panic. Again and again, he brings us face to face with a barred window: beyond is hope, but we shall never know it; so it was to be young and to be trapped in Warsaw during the last days of the war. The time is out of joint. Each man must improvise his own values and illusions to fit the occasion. In a sense, suicide may be honourable, the one way out. It feels wrong in fact to think of Jasio's last and redeeming stand as a defeat.

This improvised morality of war is neither Catholic nor Marxist; it recalls, rather, Joseph Conrad and his Lord Jim. In 1961, long after he had finished the trilogy, Wajda was encouraged to return to its themes and to make a film about the destruction of the Ghetto. The result was the beautiful, elegaic *Samson*. Though it lacks the intensity of the trilogy (so that some critics are tempted to describe it as cold), *Samson* has many virtues. It evokes the war more as a hallucination than a nightmare in a series of extraordinary images – some of them wonderfully modulated in their contrast of light and shade. And yet these image patterns are never formalist, never like those in Rossellini's *Il Generale delle Rovere* (1959), which also shows the German occupation as a hallucinatory experience. Wajda appears to feel sympathy for his protagonist, Jacob Gold; he is not detached. At the same time, he doesn't identify with him. He is at one remove from the war experience of the trilogy, and is free to explore its morality in greater depth.

By an accident Jacob kills a fellow student in an anti-semitic demonstration that turns against himself. He is jailed. (If he had been non-Jewish he would have probably been acquitted of murder.) War breaks out and again, by accident, there is a jail break. Jacob is freed. But almost at once he is swept into the Ghetto. Again, almost arbitrarily, he escapes; and is confined once more – in a flat, in a coal cellar – by various friends who wish to protect him.

179

Jacob is really without freedom. His life is arranged by others, both by the Philistines and his too friendly Dalilah. How can he regain his dignity? His own wish is to return to the Ghetto and to die with his own people. (His mother has told him that the living have above all one duty: to bury the dead.) But the Ghetto is destroyed during his captivity in the coal cellar, and when he returns to it in a blinding light he discovers a waste land. He is presented with one more choice. Some German soldiers are searching a warehouse and are about to discover a concealed printing press. Jacob, like Jasio, chooses the way of death and honour – he releases a bunch of hand grenades, and brings down the temple.

Wajda's stoicism is emotionally narrow. (But then, stoicism is usually so.) Extreme situations, though they may be powerful, call for a limited response: we must die for our honour, if not for others. It is a dismal lesson. In the final shot of *Samson* the camera pans over the dust-covered corpses of soldiers, mutilated pigeons and of Jacob, his face softened by fulfilment. This shot supposedly quietens us to a death so noble; yet I don't feel quietened. Rather, I suspect an element of spite in this ethic of honour. 'Life is like a house of cards,' says Drewnowski in *Ashes and Diamonds*; and Jacob's Dalilah actually does build such a house which he topples over accidentally. In war, perhaps, one may be forced to pull down the temple; but what of peace? Wajda offers us no alternative. Will life seem like a pack of cards when the war is over? Wajda might claim that he cannot tell, because Poland has not yet fully recovered its national identity.

The rest of us may think of extreme situations as unusual, and record them in a trembling hand. Not so Wajda. For him the extreme situation is a basis for experience, and against it all art and life must be measured. Style arises out of a knowledge of death; its values only come into being when the mind has been strengthened wonderfully. It is for this reason that his art of crisis can afford to be so elegantly wrought.

Samson is a comment on war. But the trilogy is the real furnace – the living enactment: an art of the moment in which the present dilates and spreads, obliterating past and future; an art finding expression more in the shock of image, than in the continuity and time sequence of plot. 'Naturalism,' says Wajda, 'is the opposite of my intentions – because what I aim at is the creation of isolated and intense moments with no attempt at observing the principle of probability.' He claims to be influenced by Buñuel's *L'Age d'Or*; and some of his images, such as the slow motion shot of the dying man falling into the chapel at the opening of *Ashes and Diamonds*, have the detached intensity of, say, those Buñuel close-ups, so cool and deliberate, of scorpions fighting each other to death. Even so, Wajda is far from being a surrealist. His art is one of the mind in extreme stress and not in reverie. I am reminded of Eisenstein's *coup de poing* theory of montage. There is the same calculated attempt to shock, the same distraction by image. But Wajda is not really concerned with propaganda or with working out a latent sadism – though he may, like Eisenstein, lack a belief in some sustaining goodness. His trilogy is a personal testament, and his shocks are an essential part of the experience it communicates.

What happens, though, is that these war experiences are put over with such a natural power that they become totally convincing. We see them as a basis against which the events of daily life will appear grotesque. In the context of war, a white wedding or the photographer's cardboard heart outside a church look ridiculous. Wajda likes to make us smile at the grotesque, then twists our arm. The boys steal a truck and scatter its cargo of hissing geese out on to the road; a few moments later we are drawn into Jasio's chase. Or again, the boys steal coal from a train. It is like a game – *jeux interdits* – until one of them is shot.

Wajda gives the immediate impression. He is indifferent, even contemptuous, of historical truth. In *A Generation*, the resistance fighters under orders from London are caricatured with the venom of an Eisenstein. In *Kanal*, the evidence is falsified. It was partisans under orders from London, and not the Communists shown by Wajda, who were driven into the sewers. The Communists and the Russian army (on the other side of the Vistula) were ordered to stay out of the battle until the insurgents were wiped out. Perhaps Wajda had to make these misrepresentations to satisfy the Party, or perhaps (unlikely) he was misinformed. At any rate, he might claim it to be of little relevance. The trilogy acts as a denial of historical truth. Intellectually, when seen as a whole, it is nihilist. Wajda's one belief appears to be in the power of art to re-create life on the pulse, its power to revive feeling by compression.

The form of *Ashes and Diamonds* shows this clearly. On the level of history, it denies all laws. It opens with the murder of a wrong man, moves through a series of muddles and mis- understandings, and ends with the accidental shooting of its hero. History is on the side of nobody, is mere contingency. (It is interesting that Maciek's death should be similar to the murder of Michel in Godard's *A Bout de Souffle* (1960).) The Marxist theory of history does no more than turn everything into ashes, grey and dull. The pretentious Sekula has gone, and in his place is the worn-out Party secretary, Szczuka, who in Andrzejewski's novel played a major role, but who is as in- effectual as a lost terrier in the film. Against him is placed Maciek, a hero as 'brilliant' as a diamond, all glittering hard surfaces. In time, though, the ashes reclaim the diamond. Maciek sinks and is lost.

Wajda's plot is as 'brilliant' as his hero; and his taut, articulate form also comes off best when compared with the incoherence of history. Much use is made of coincidence, of epiphanies, of dazzling recognitions. Most of the action takes place in a hotel – the Monopole – an ideal place for bringing together many characters with diverse intentions. This action affects us like a kaleidoscope: it shakes up a continuous change of patterns. Through a bewildering concourse of meetings the characters reveal different facets of themselves. As the various factions jostle for power, the Monopole becomes a microcosm of Poland on the last day of the war.

Yet in what sense is the hotel a microcosm? Before us is the flux of metropolitan life – and the question of how these innumerable facts are to be ordered into a significant form. Hitchcock's *Rear Window* (1953) has a similar location to *Ashes and Diamonds* – a block of flats surrounded by a courtyard – and there is a similar impression of many lives related in an arbitrary manner. But Hitchcock doesn't *impose* a form, doesn't see his courtyard as a microcosm of New York and its inhabitants as representative of this city, as did King Vidor in *Street Scene* (1930). His form, rather, is given shape by a governing consciousness. Relationships exist mainly in the mind of the injured photographer confined to his room, watching the antics of his neighbours as impassively as a camera; by implication, we are meant to see things through his eyes. This observer only becomes actor in his own room, in his relationships with fiancée, nurse or friend. There is a contrast (brought out especially in the treatment of sound effects) between the observed action of people outside – amusing, pathetic, macabre – and the intense claustrophobic involvements in the room. But as usual in a Hitchcock film the distinction between observer and actor soon breaks down. The hero is presently drawn into a nightmare in which he feels he is struggling against the whole world. (Rabbit holes abound in the Hitchcock landscape, and they seldom lead to Wonderland.) It is only then, as the photographer is briefly caught up in the action, that *Rear Window* comes close to *Ashes and Diamonds*. Maciek may look across the hotel courtyard and see Slomka, the proprietor, bullying a woman in the room opposite; but this is one of the few scenes where he is an observer. Indeed, it would be inaccurate to think of him as a governing consciousness or as being at the centre of the action. All the actors have an equal relevance to the action, and all of them do *act*. Even the toilet attendant is involved in the business of handing out lavatory paper or of mopping the floor. If she, Slomka, or Pieniozek, the journalist, appear as grotesque, they do so on Wajda's principle that the less people's actions have to do with the serious conflicts of war, the more grotesque they become.

But what are these important conflicts? The form of *Ashes and Diamonds* is dramatic (rather than novelistic); it is also deceptive. There is an action – yet what is it about exactly? The characters act – yet to what end? The times are out of joint; and we are reminded of *Hamlet*, where enterprises of great pith and moment lose the name of action. Maciek comes to the hotel to kill Szczuka, falls in love and loses the impulse to murder, though shortly he does commit it. As Hadelin Trinon shows,* the futility of his actions is parodied by his *alter ego* Drewnowski, whose scandal at the banquet, when he sprays the guests with a fire extinguisher, and his disgrace when he is thrown down stairs, mime Maciek's machine-gunning of the wrong man and his ignominious death. Ideological concerns are absent and political issues are glided over. Private matters confuse with the public interest. Even the politically committed Szczuka is absorbed in the worry of not knowing his son's whereabouts.

Yet in spite of its episodic action, *Ashes and Diamonds* has a deeply satisfying form that embraces the content and enriches its meaning. How so? How is Wajda able to transcend the naturalism of, say, Vidor's *Street Scene*? The answer is simple: by an almost flagrant use of coincidence. In the hotel people are brought together and swept apart as though merely servants to the plot. Maciek and Szczuka pass each other a number of times, and Maciek lights Szczuka's cigarette on two occasions. Coincidences may be the obverse to the accidental event; yet they are merely the different sides to the same coin. And this coin is the basic exchange in the economy of *Ashes and Diamonds*.

It would be tempting to see Wajda's use of coincidence as no

* Andrzej Wajda: *Cinéma d'Aujourd'hui*, 1964.

more than conventional, such as we find it in Jacques Demy's *Lola* (1960). Demy is as witty as Feydeau in bringing together his characters in a denial of all possibility. He makes a virtue of accident. His form is imposed; his themes interweave music-ally; and the *deus ex machina* bobs up graciously everywhere, to the applause and gratitude of its victims. In *La Baie des Anges* (1962), though, Demy puts such a happy belief in fate to the test. His roulette-playing heroine is continually raising prayers to the Allah of fate; yet as the events show, her changing logic of luck is no more than a series of rationalizations – attempts to justify her gambling impulse. The coincidences in *Ashes and Diamonds* are more than plot convention; they are an essential part of its content. However, Wajda doesn't expect us to believe in fate. In his work there is no *deus ex machina* or imminent God. Yet the murderer needs his victim as a son needs his father; and, by implication, the victim needs his murderer as a father needs his son. Poland is like a family torn apart by Civil War. Once there was order. Once there were sympathies. But these have been disturbed. All the same, though the family has broken apart, it is natural that the parts should be drawn together – natural that Szczuka should call round on Mme Staniewicz, an old friend, whose husband (though he doesn't know it) is now his antagonist. People are drawn to each other like iron filings to a magnet. Their need for each other may lead to a mutual destruction, but this hazard must be put down to the circumstances of war, and not to the need itself. When Maciek shoots Szczuka, the old man falls into his arms. At the same moment fireworks blaze in the sky in celebration of victory, and are reflected in a puddle near to the two men.

We are mirror images to each other. Wajda's coincidences are warmed by his belief in men's reciprocity. The world of *Ashes and Diamonds* is like a field of influences, deflecting the characters from their intended course, opening them to new encounters and fresh, often confusing revelations. People are like balls on a pin table, nudged from pin to pin as they roll downwards. Maciek and Krystyna have made love. They go

185

for a walk. In a bombed church they come across a poem by Cyprion Norwid, carved on a wall. *Lost beneath the ashes a diamond shines with all its brilliance like a dawn announcing victory* . . . 'Who are we?' asks Krystyna, and Maciek answers, 'The diamond – that's you.' Before them, creaking and groaning, swings an upturned crucifix with Christ still on the Cross. Krystyna breaks the heel on one of her shoes, and Maciek takes the shoe into a chapel and tries to mend it with a communion bell; then he removes a dust sheet from two corpses lying there and discovers the two men he had murdered that morning. Krystyna screams.

The poem, the crucifix, the corpses – these are not symbols but arbitrary influences, pressures even, on Maciek's mind. The one thing they have in common is to push him back into the past and make him face the feelings he would prefer to forget. There is always a movement back to a former order, and ridicule won't save us from it. The Polonaise may be butchered by an indifferent pianist, yet it still remains Chopin's Polonaise. If Wajda is at all an optimist, he is so here in his hinted-at theme that national identity cannot be suppressed. History may lie, yet there is a coherence beyond history that the artist, in spite of censorship, must seek out. The closely knit plot both affirms the random nature of events *and* gives shape to Wajda's vision of an order beneath the flux.

This vision of an order can be summarized in one phrase: a generation. In his trilogy Wajda spoke for his generation, indeed for one cycle of life. Now his generation is middle-aged and, I suspect, disillusioned. The promise of the Resistance and the new regime is betrayed. Wajda has spoken for that promise and its heroism, and perhaps now he has little more to say; the relative slackness of *Lotna* and *Siberian Lady Macbeth* would suggest so. On the evidence of *Innocent Sorcerers* (1960) and his sketch in *Love at Twenty* (1962) he appears to be bitter towards the younger generation, as though sensing his dislodgement. 'In *Love at Twenty*,' he says, 'I tried to show my feelings

about these young people I don't understand and don't like.'
He feels much the same way about the young people in *Innocent
Sorcerers*, and claims to be alienated by their cynicism. Both he
and Tadeusz Lomnicki, who plays the hero (he also plays
Stach in *A Generation*, incredible though it may seem), ap-
proached their task coldly.

I wonder, though, how seriously we should take Wajda's
disapproval. In *Ashes and Diamonds* Zbigniew Cybulski as
Maciek wore dark glasses and the Western style clothes which
apparently were favoured by the young Polish rebels of the
fifties. And Wajda is still a young man (he was born in 1926),
though from the way he talks you would think he was aged
seventy. Possibly a fear of censorship forces him into expressing
disapproval. Andrzej, the hero of *Innocent Sorcerers*, is flam-
boyantly, *dangerously* pro-Western. He plays jazz, drinks inferior
gin masked in a bottle of *Gordon's Dry*, has a portrait of
Einstein over his gas-ring, and above all wants to visit Paris
and the United States. He may be frivolous and 'cool', all that
Wajda condemns; but then so were the aristocrats at Eisenstein's
Polish court. Andrzej is incurably Polish – elegant, witty, and
subtle – and nowhere more so than when he is flirting with girls.
He plays at life as though it were a game, until he meets his
match in a girl named Magda. (Both of them, significantly,
prefer to travel incognito and call each other by nicknames:
Basile and Pelagie.) Their moment of truth, and the centrepiece
of the film, is a game of strip poker. Afraid of the emotions
they feel for each other, they both try to keep up their defences.
But they fail. They stumble. Their style breaks apart. In spite of
Wajda's claims, he cannot help showing these two people as
likable. Their poise is precarious; and beneath it, one imagines,
they are as honourable as the generation that fought in the
Resistance. No doubt if those days were to return they would
behave in much the same way as their predecessors did – and I
cannot help feeling that Wajda believes this also.

Satyajit Ray

The success of a myth can be gauged by its power to control the mind, so that a partial reality seems to contain the whole truth. China, for instance, was inaccessible too long to stir up such a myth in the British mind. In recent times Cathay has never been more than an affectation, a delightful and autonomous kingdom in fairyland. A vogue like chinoiserie could proliferate because it was, so obviously, a European invention.*
In comparison, the effect of India has been more deeply felt. It has its myth, and the affectation failed. In spite of the Prince Regent's wish for a 'Hindoo' temple, indiennerie has never really taken root in this country. Nobody believed in 'fabulous Ind'. India was Empire, explored, subjugated, and somehow known. And yet not known. For India, we are told, remains a living mystery. In the post-Kipling phase this knowing has sometimes taken the form of a loving revulsion. 'Indians defecate everywhere. They defecate, mostly, besides the railway tracks. But they also defecate on the beaches; they defecate on the hills; they defecate on the river banks; they defecate on streets; they never look for cover.'

V. S. Naipaul's *An Area of Darkness* is the most impressive of recent descriptions, although it doesn't alter radically the myth created by E. M. Forster. A sense of disequilibrium, of

* According to Hugh Honour, its creator was not so much Marco Polo as 'Sir John Mandeville' – who 'has a claim to fame as a perpetrator of the most successful fraud in the whole history of literature, since his book had been translated into ten languages and was well known for five hundred years before it was proved that Sir John Mandeville had never existed, his travels never taken place and his "personal experiences" were mere plagiarisms and inventions.' (*Chinoiserie*. Murray 1961.)

anger, of a despair that subdues irony – in Naipaul's account at least, the myth dwindles down to a response barely supported by facts. I don't know how far it measures up to the truth; and as an armchair traveller who cherishes his dreams too much actually to travel, I'm in no position to say. But I am sceptical. Naipaul's India fits in too well with the accepted present-day model of reality; it has the obligatory bitter tang.

Does Satyajit Ray, on the other hand, create a more per-suasive image of India? If Naipaul's account is accurate, then we shall be forced to see Ray's work as being like Forster's Aziz – as charming and graceful, but also as irresponsible and, ultimately, as escapist. But even by his life alone, Ray manages to dent Naipaul's myth . . .

The making of *Pather Panchali* is a heroic story, often told: how a thirty-one year old commercial artist with no practical experience of the cinema set out in 1952 to direct a script based on a widely-read novel by Bibhati Banerji. The problems were formidable and never-ending: a lack of equipment and funds; the need to film hectically over weekends and holidays – Ray was still working for the Keymar advertising agency; the race against time to complete the film for its first showing at the Museum of Modern Art, New York; and, eventually, the battle to have it shown at Cannes (1956); the scandal because some of the jury missed the screening – who could have anticipated a masterpiece from Bengal? – and the winning of a major prize.

Since that time Ray has directed over eight feature films. The best of these – the trilogy, for example – enchant me to such a degree that I find it hard to write about them. Again, I suspect the oppressive sway of myth. 'There is no reason,' says Ray, 'why we should not cash in on the foreigner's curiosity about the Orient. But this doesn't mean pandering to his love of the false-exotic. A great many notions about our country and people have to be dispelled, even though it may be easier and more paying to sustain existing myths.' A dialogue with the British, especially, runs through his work. In *Pather Panchali* a village brass band plays *Colonel Bogey*, embellished by many an atonal grace-note. In *Two Daughters* (1961) a lunatic resembling Robinson Crusoe struts about stiffly like a soldier of the Raj – *left, right, left, right*! Though seldom more than hinted at, the British inheritance is always present; though the British – save for a sympathetic, etiolated Anglo-Indian girl in *Mahanagar* (1963) and a glimpse of them in *Kachenjunga* (1962) – remain a haunting absence. Ray's feelings about this burdensome past are amiable. He only allows resentment to break through in his documentary, *Rabindranath Tagore* (1961), in the repeated newsclip of British soldiers laying into rioters with batons.

But the enchantment of Ray's work, the suspected myth, lies less in this personal dialogue with us than in his image of private life: the tenderness of his lovers, the tired civility of the older generation, the charm of his children. Similar touches are to be found in *Bicycle Thieves* and everywhere in Renoir, but Ray brings to them his own warmth, his own insights. He takes his own time in tracing the curlicues of intimacy. But such a balance is sustained perilously; generosity can spill over into indulgence. Isn't Ray's view of the unworldly Apu a bit too tolerant? Doesn't the charm of the family in *Devi* (1960) – though they are aristocrats – come over as a little too precious? Further flaws seem to appear as we turn the jewel. Ray's vision is limited: he is not concerned with evil in the Western sense, nor does he rely on those staple ingredients of the commercial cinema – lust, murder and rape. His protagonists are never brutes. His work, in short, lacks the obligatory bitter tang.

Crudely, this may be true. But all the same, without being emphatic, Ray does show us the dark side to human nature. The child Apu points an arrow thoughtfully at the hopeless, panting family dog. Cruelty may take the form of negligence – yet its effects can often be as painful as any of those in a more lurid tale. Apu's grandmother is neglected and crawls away to die; only then do the family begin to realize what they have done to her. Well-to-do children, showing off their toys and sweets, taunt Apu and his sister for their poverty. Wickedness is casual. Mr Nanda, in *Two Daughters*, can't stand running a jungle post office: his neighbours play excruciating music, he is teased by a fearful lunatic and he catches malaria. So he goes. But he leaves behind a child whom he was teaching the alphabet, and who had centred her life on serving him. Mr Nanda escapes at the expense of destroying the hopeful child – for no one else will save her from outpost life. Ray doesn't blame; he merely records. And, anyway, how was the amiable Mr Nanda to know the extent of his carelessness? Evil is seldom positive. A heavy father stunts his children in *Kachenjunga*, a nonchalant husband almost destroys his wife in *Mahanaghar*. Intimacy magnifies; in family life a mere slight can cut deep. Ray works on this microscopic scale; he takes the greatest risks – and, really, it is surprising how seldom he misjudges the tone.

Why so seldom? Because he doesn't impose on his characters; they respond to him; they have their own resilience. Ray is able wonderfully to create the sort of situation that develops under its own momentum. There is a sense of separate life. In the second part of *Two Daughters* a young law student, as self-centred as Mr Nanda, decides to marry a wild tomboy, Puglee, against her will. Conventions being what they are, she has to submit. But on the wedding night she slips away to her childhood toys: a swing by a river, a ruined shrine, a squirrel in a cage. A row breaks out when the student's mother learns that the marriage hasn't been consummated; neighbours are scandalized; Puglee is locked up in her husband's bedroom and smashes up the furniture. Then, gradually, the lovers begin to get through to each other. Egotism dissolves. Some sort of harmony is established. The individual is limited; he cannot hope to redirect the broad river of life to suit his own purpose. In an arrogant director such a vision would be pessimistic. But Ray *accepts* diversity. The courtyard in *Pather Panchali* is like a painting by Carpaccio: a dog chews scraps, a cat lazes in the sun, a goose struts about purposefully and now and then honks. The father scribbles at his manuscripts, Apu is up to his jokes, and the grandmother talks to herself. Only the mother frets and nags and tries to order everything – a tragic figure. In spite of poverty and waste, Ray is an optimist.

He is in love with nuance, with the subtle shifting relationship of people to each other and to Nature; because of this, it is hard to pin down the source of his dynamism, the grain in the oyster. His view of things is immediate, iridescent. Moments from his earlier films confuse in the mind with recollections of our own past; they have the rich compression of memory. *Aux yeux du souvenir que le monde est petit*! A sweetseller is seen across water and through sunny trees; a school inspector's buggy rides along by a river bed to the dry rattle of a *tabla* – haunting moments, inexplicably so. Yet like all great directors, Ray's work is consistent. His impressions have the unity of growth and develop out of a central theme. This theme argues itself out far beneath the surface, and only emerges (as in *Devi*) when the surface runs thin. The trouble about defining this theme is that, once defined, it makes his work – above all the trilogy – sound too schematic.

'In what way can man control the world, and what is the price he must pay for doing so?' ... I'm in no position to say whether this theme grew out of Ray's own experience – though the story of the trilogy does bear some relation to his life: the early death of his gifted father, poverty, the dislocation of the move to stay with his mother's family. But it does relate to politics. To describe this poet of intimacy as politically conscious may sound odd; still, as he shows us, in India the intimate verges into the public. It needs locked doors, winter evenings and a reasonable income to make the two distinguishable. In Ray's India neighbours are always nudging in to share the tragedy or the pickings. The lovers in *Devi* require privacy, and the camera holds back; a kiss is seen in middle distance and in silhouette. But the wife goes mad in public and runs away through streams of sunlight. In *Kachenjunga* the most crucial dilemmas are worked out in a park or on a main road. In *Mahanaghar* the city mob join in the uproar at the collapse of a private bank. But Ray's theme is political in a more obvious sense. It is closely related to the fact of India's coming to Independence in 1947.

Independence brought autonomy of a sort to India – but at the cost of terrible massacres. Change was necessary, yet its demands undermined. Mechanization, and the attempts to modernize agriculture destroyed ancient pieties. The India of science was pitted against the India of myths. According to Naipaul, the battle is as good as lost. The past is too obdurate; like the jungle it regains its hold and pulls everything down. There is a confusion of loyalties. Vacillation prevails. Ray shares in this uncertainty; he, too, is restrained by the past. The trilogy is removed from a sense of time, since the contemporary problems it deals with are blurred by being set in the past. Again, the subject of *Devi* is the urgent one of religious super-stition. Yet Ray tempers his attack by putting back the action by a hundred years. Maybe he hoped to damp down the ire of Hindu fundamentalists – in which case he failed; for *Devi* caused such a scandal that it was refused an export certificate for a long time. But his motive was probably less conscious. Ray's sense of time, perhaps luckily for him, is different from ours. He is disposed to think in terms of myth; and in *Apu Sansar* (1958) at least, he reverts consciously to this circular mode of thinking.

Things sink back into torpor; the struggle is too great. The ageing nobleman in *Jalsaghar* (1958) finds himself out of place in the modern world. He tries to escape into the world of music. But he fails. The thunder of trucks on their way to a factory owned by his newly-rich neighbour echoes through his palace. *Jalsaghar* strips bare a dying world. The nobleman is trapped and alone; and his palace is a mausoleum, lost in an unending parched desert. Far away stands an immobile elephant. The trucks pass, and a great chandelier shivers in one of the marble saloons. On the flat roof the nobleman, that other pachyderm, smokes his hookah and meditates, while nearby strut doves. He appears to have forgotten his dead family. Or, possibly, their death drove him into this land of dreams. He is separated from the terrace below by wire netting, through which, sometimes, he and his one remaining servant call back and forth to each other lazily. The old panjandrum is selfish, a bloated lizard; yet he has dignity – an oddly moving figure. And the way he ruins himself is pleasing, not by the usual vices, but by a passion for private concerts. I doubt, though, whether he is quite the last representative of the old world that Ray presumably meant him to be. The epitaph was a little premature, and the satire could have more edge. But Ray's talents don't lie in this direction; he is too sensitive to the feelings of others. His comment, if you could call it such, comes through his awareness of vitality in people and things. There is no point in ridiculing the nobleman. Life is so obviously ebbing out of him.

Oppression and liberation; death as a withdrawal, life as a burgeoning: the action oscillates between these polarities. Women, awakened to their rights, blossom at the chance of freedom. The beautiful Doyamoyee in *Devi* isn't allowed to be free; she is turned into a Goddess, a thing, and goes mad. Arati, the wife in *Mahanagar* has a taste for emancipation – takes a job, uses lipstick, and finds herself. But she, too, virtually sacrifices herself when she learns she is a more capable money-earner than her husband. 'In what way can man control the world?' Ray, a man of the new world, is on the side of the liberators – of people, like Apu, who try to break away from superstition and ignorance. But he doesn't neglect to show how you need to be ruthless to carry out such a struggle, and how, at times, the conflict may deaden feeling. Apu betrays his mother's affection by leaving her to die alone in a remote village; and later, as a man of learning, begins to lose touch with life – with Mother Earth, as he puts it – to his natural detriment. To escape from despair may mean to numb oneself, to escape into the prison of egotism.

A great deal of *Pather Panchali* is taken up with showing the condition of people who have lost out. Most of them are fatalists – and perhaps because of this they are still able to enjoy them-

selves. The tone is set in the opening sequence: a child ineffec-
tually sweeps a sunbaked courtyard, kittens frolic in the shade.
There is a strong feeling of family unity. Senses are sharp and
alert. Life is lived at its most primitive, biological level. Food
is the main concern: the mother never seems to stop crushing
harsh roots; the children steal fruit or yearn for sweets they
cannot afford; the grandmother loudly gobbles in a corner. The
family are always eating – scraps of rice, rotting guavas, pieces
of sugar cane.

They are exposed to the fury of Nature. When Renoir was
filming *The River* near Calcutta, Ray had the chance to watch
several days' location shooting. Renoir encouraged his plan to
make *Pather Panchali*, and also appears to have transmitted
something of his feeling for Nature. For Ray, Nature is both
lovely and terrible: waterflies flick exquisitely over the lotus
pond as the monsoon approaches. In Renoir's *The Southerner*
(1945) an intemperate climate and an infrangible soil almost
break the pioneer family. Renoir knows that Nature can destroy
completely; at the same time, he never forgets that she is a
major source of goodness, and his tracking shots across the
tobacco fields are as tender as a caress. So, in *Pather Panchali*,
the jungle can be both a child's paradise and a predator; finally,
it creeps through a broken wall and devours the courtyard. The
monsoon beats down the house and, after the family have left,
a snake slides across the broken pavings. The family is defence-
less; almost everything, and everybody, is against them.
Neighbours are rapacious. Education at the hand of the village
grocer seems a futile preparation for life. Primitive medicine is
no prophylactic against disease. Death is both frequent and
unexpected. (Not surprisingly, Ray has long wanted to film
A Passage to India.) The world is uncontrollable, and the family
– each in its own way – is at its mercy. The father, a gentle dis-
tracted egoist, dreams of his ancestors' greatness but is unable
to make a living. His employers cheat him and he writes plays
nobody wants. The mother – inarticulate conscience of the
family – is the only one to achieve some sort of control over

events. But even she fails, and the failure shows in her continual scrubbing and scraping and nagging, which cuts her off more and more from the others. Then there is the grandmother, who never despairs though she has no reason for hope. It isn't in gloom but with wry joy that she says, 'I am old and have nowhere to go'. Unlike Gorki's grandmother who is an earth-goddess embodying (as one of the revolutionaries puts it) the best of Old Russia, she is never more than likably irresponsible.

The difference between the Ray and the Gorki trilogy (as filmed by Mark Donskoi) can be seen in these two women. Gorki is concerned with the drama of Revolution and with showing how his characters, even at second hand, react to it. Ray isn't primarily interested in such a drama. He is more concerned with understanding the world than with changing it; though to understand the world may possibly bring about a change. His comment on social progress remains ambiguous, often aggravatingly so. The difference between these two trilogies isn't necessarily antagonistic; it is the difference, one might say, between the zestful Russia of the late twenties and the neutralist India of the fifties.

Anyhow, the characters of *Pather Panchali* could never bring about a Revolution even if they wanted to; they are all too much like children. It may be a brilliant touch to have all the characters like children in a film about a child, and so to relate a pastoral community to the limitations of this age group, but it does induce a certain ambiguity of vision. Doubts arise. Are we, or are we not, seeing the action through the eyes of a child? Ray never resolves this question. Happily, this confusion of time works for him. The experience operates on two levels, slipping back and forth; it resists definition and continues to tease the mind. Also plot saves the action from monotony – plot, and the way in which each member of the family plays a part unobtrusively in developing the main theme.

There is the pivotal moment, for instance, when Apu sees a train for the first time and begins to understand the extent of man's power. (Trains are a recurring idea in the trilogy, and this scene takes on an added force when we remember how later, in Calcutta, Apu is to try and commit suicide by throwing himself beneath one.) The sequence is short; and yet, by its build-up, dominates the film. Apu and his sister move through the wilderness of a cotton field. Seeds drift from white plumes. They listen to the eerie humming of telephone wires. Then the train chatters past, its smoke obliterating the sky like a dusky feather. All quite usual to us perhaps; but for Apu a Mechanical Messiah is born. We recall an earlier scene at twilight, the house in darkness. The short-sighted grandmother is trying to thread a needle but is too proud to admit failure. Near her the mother fusses alone. The father stops trying to write a play and, holding up a moth-eaten bundle of manuscripts, says gently, 'Things have come to a pretty pass.' Beside him Apu is learning to write, and the father smiles at the success of his work. Far off, a passing train whistles. 'Now,' says the father, 'write the word for wealth.'

The comic travelling theatre, the father's escapism, the grand-mother's folklore gleam poignantly in the obscurity of this hopeless situation. The mother, trying to control a dwindling budget, goes out and sells the family silver; but the price she pays is to rob Apu of his patrimony and to destroy the lingering remains of a family tradition. This theme of control and its cost is all important in Ray's work; yet against it there is an almost mystical belief in the power of life itself, a notion which is to play a large part in *Apu Sansar*. Here at least it is hinted at in the scene when the grandmother rocks the new-born Apu in his cradle. She looks at him with hope, though she fears for his future; and this mingled regard reveals both her wisdom and strength. In the last resort, the terror of Nature's destruction is mitigated by the knowledge that life continues.

The family may be defeated by the jungle, yet *Pather Panchali* isn't a film about defeat. Apu's sister dies, and he throws her necklace into a fetid pond. As the algae close around the necklace and the pond swallows the last trace of his sister's existence, we might be tempted to think, 'ah well, in time death obliterates us all'. Then we remember that the girl had stolen the necklace. Apu has thrown it away to cover her tracks and to preserve her idealized memory. This moment, then, is ironical; notwithstanding its pathos, it keeps us from being sentimental.

In spite of death and destruction, what we mainly remember from this film are its glowing images of passing bands and rickshaws, of children running through sunlit glades, and of trains – especially trains – with their hope of work in Benares and their promise of a new and better society. The English translation for *Pather Panchali* is, aptly, *On the Road*. It is, above all else, the activity of life that counts. As one of the villagers sagely remarks, 'it's staying in one place that makes you mean.'

And now the growing Apu begins to control the world. A premonition of this in *Pather Panchali*, when he first saw the train, is confirmed by the pivotal moment in *Aparajito* (1956) when a shot of the boy triumphantly holding a small globe is followed by a glimpse of his home-made sundial. Time and space have begun to be conquered.

Aparajito is an indecisive film. There is little plot, merely a series of episodes related to each other by the most tenuous of connections. Typical of this disorder is the restless shifting of location: Benares and the father's death, Dejaphur, a village, Calcutta, and another village – it is all very fragmentary. Ray goes in for sensationalist cutting and for an obvious sort of symbolism as though he were trying to cover up his incoherence. Even the pathetic fallacy, of all things, is dragged in at one moment; as the father dies, pigeons scatter over the city.

The problem in making a sequel to a well-plotted film is of finding another plot for the same characters which, without strain, will develop them. In *Aparajito* Apu has become the protagonist, but he has neither the personality of a child nor the complexity of an adult to sustain the role. He has become a rather weedy adolescent, seen in middle distance, whose problems are beyond the range of Ray's fastidious talent. The mother, edged into the centre of the action, doesn't fulfil the new demands made on her. In *Pather Panchali* she was never more than a form of conscience, nagging away like the toothache. Ray is unable to develop her into a major character, and really is unable to do anything with her. In consequence he forces the scenes in which she appears. At her death, expressionistic techniques run riot. The camera veers over walls and lingers on flames. The confusion is general. We never learn why the mother is allowed to die alone; or whether we are supposed to see the final scene through her eyes. But *Aparajito* doesn't fail totally. It is saved, in part, by a number of Ray vignettes, such as the school inspector who admires Apu's prompt answers and who bestows on him a benign smile, or the bed-sitter bachelor who lends the boy a box of matches so as to have the chance to make a pass at his mother. *Aparajito* just manages to hold our interest between the earlier masterpiece of *Pather Panchali* and the later, probably finer, *Apu Sansar*.

How was Ray able to save his trilogy? In part, by relying no longer on Banerji's novel. Unconstrained, his style becomes more fluent. What does it mean to have life moving through you? The theme touched on in *Panther Panchali* is here faced directly. Apu gives up his study of science to become a writer; but he is over-selfconscious, feels nothing, is a living death. He is all he was not as a child. 'He doesn't make it,' he tells his friend Pulu, speaking of a character in his novel but referring unknowingly to himself. 'Still, he doesn't turn away from life. He faces up to reality.' *Apu Sansar*, then, is self-reflexive; we are fascinated to see how Ray will have *us* face up to reality as he makes his hero return to the vital world he has denied, of childhood and the village.

Ray brings out vividly Apu's remoteness from experience. Pulu invites Apu to a wedding in the country and tells him in an affectionately mocking tone of the old world village where it is to take place; at once Ray cuts to a panning shot of Apu walking along an embankment chanting a poem. 'Let me return to thy lap, O Earth! . . . Free me from the prison of my mind . . .' Apu, indeed, is caught in the prison of his own mind. Divorced from the industrial society about him, he lives locked away in his garret with his onanistic flute playing and his (of all things) autobiographical novel. People enter this room as if they had come to some foreign land.

But this omniscience is soon jolted. The bridegroom at the country wedding turns out to be roaring mad. Custom requires the bride to be married within twenty-four hours, or else be cursed by bad luck. The parents in despair turn to Apu, and he, despairingly, submits to them. The marriage takes place – and so begins the happiest period in Apu's life. But happiness ends just as randomly. His wife dies in childbirth. Enclosed in his room, Apu is obliterated by grief and resentment at the child whom (he thinks) killed his wife. He leaves Calcutta. A beard has grown during his time of mourning, and he now resembles a pilgrim. He wanders through the countryside, and finds incomprehensible the reality he had once thought himself superior to. He had believed learning gave him some sort of order – in one of his books he kept a dried fern leaf – that he had somehow categorized the world. And yet, as he moves sadly through a forest, he comes across a cluster of ferns and is shocked by their mysterious otherness. His novel, he realizes, is miserable; he had misunderstood everything, absolutely everything. Unable to carry on as a creative being, he withdraws from life. Much later, in his first encounter with his five year old son, he understands his mistake. By his presence the boy acts as a criticism of Apu and calls him back to his neglected duties as a father. Apu needs this child with his unselfconscious vitality, and through him begins to return to sanity.

This plot takes on the intensity of myth. As he sails with Pulu down a river to the old world village, Apu chants, 'Where are you taking us, O Fair One?' The boatman, thinking he is being referred to, smiles. But Apu is tricked by his own irony, for he is unaware that the fair river is leading him directly to his as yet unknown wife. The river is always there in the background, reminding us of nature both as an arbitrary yet regenerative power. The river is there when Apu decides to marry, or – now shrunken to a stream – when Pulu tries to pull him back to life after four years of grief, or when he and his son are reconciled. A riverscape with figures, then, in which neither dwarfs the other and in which both are usually present.

On the heights of myth, the plot tells of a god's death and resurrection. Apu is, perhaps, an avatar of the flute-playing god, Krishna. Certainly, they have much in common. This god, you will remember, was allowed for a while to love a milkmaid called Radha; similarly, Apu is allowed to love his wife Aparna. But again, only for a brief time. After her death Apu descends into a landscape of salt where he is imprisoned with his own echo. (His sacredness is sick, even though he may have the aspect of a holy man. Unexpectedly, Ray shows little sympathy for those who seek spiritual contemplation at the expense of duty.) *Apu Sansar* reminds us of how true myth is the silt of time, an accretion of wisdom. Nature renews itself so completely that each spring is like its predecessor. The power of time is honed by repetition. Children find themselves each generation by making the same discoveries, and fathers re-find themselves through their children. The theme of regeneration, no more than hinted at in *Pather Panchali*, is here articulated sharply. And so, when Apu returns to the village – it might be the village where he was born – and confronts his childhood self, we too feel reconciled. The trilogy has taken on circular form and rises out of time.

Ray takes a risk by making his hero an avatar of Krishna. Yet Apu's friend, Pulu, who laughs at him for his self-regard, acts as our critical balance; the suggestion of myth is never allowed to swamp the immediate experience. *Apu Sansar* does have its weaknesses: such as the violent music when one of the wedding guests says that the curse becomes a blessing (Ray may believe in magic but he doesn't commit himself), or the over-emphatic moment when Apu throws his novel away and the sheets cascade over the forest. But these faults are slight and do no harm to this beautiful masterpiece.

Index

À Bout de Souffle 182
Agee, James 22
Age d'Or, L' 181
Albertazzi, Giorgio 139
Alexander Nevsky 63
Almereyda, (Vigo *père*) 19–21
Anderson, Lindsay 75–6
Andrzejewski, Jerzy 171, 182
Anges du Péché, Les 35
Année Dernière à Marienbad, L'
 138, 139, 140, 141, 144–8
Antonioni, Michelangelo 12–13,
 46–7, 125, 142–3
Aparajito 201–2
Apollinaire, Guillaume 17, 54
À Propos de Nice 18, 20–2
Apu Sansar 196, 200, 202–5
Arendt, Hannah 13, 14, 92
Artaud, Antonin 112
Ashes and Diamonds 172–3, 177,
 180, 181, 182–6, 187
Atalante, L' 25–30
Auden, W. H. 73, 101, 122
Augustine, St. 133
Autant-Lara, Claude 45
Avventura, L' 46, 125

Bacon, Francis 62, 144
Baie des Anges, La 185
Banerji, Bibhati 192

Barbaro, Umberto 123
Battleship Potemkin 54, 62–3,
 86
Baudelaire, Charles 74
Beckett, Samuel 47
Beethoven 79, 123
Bergman, Ingmar 165
Bernstein, Henri 152
Beylie, Claude 161
Beyond the Fringe 79
Bicycle Thieves 124, 193
Bidone, Il 128
Birth of a Nation, The 11
Blake, William 67, 71, 72, 76, 110
Boccaccio '70 132
Brecht, Bertold 99, 150
Bresson, Robert 12, 35–47
BBC World War I Series 73
Bronowski, Jacob 71, 72
Brooks, Louise 167
Brownlow, Kevin 70
Buñuel, Luis 18, 24, 172, 181
Burel Léonce-Henri 39

Cabinet of Dr Caligari, The 87
Cardinale, Claudia 130
Carol, Martine 162
Casarès, Maria 142
Cayrol, Jean 149, 150
Cézanne, Paul 13

Index

Chabrol, Claude 112
Chaplin, Charles 22, 28
Chekov, Anton 122
Cherkassov, Nicolai 63
Chesney, Jasmine 142
Chesterton, G. K. 101
Chien Andalou, Le 18, 24
Citizen Kane 101, 137–9, 141, 143, 144, 153, 155, 166
Clair, René 23
Cocteau, Jean 40, 63, 104, 113
Coleman, John 131
Coleridge, S. T. 111, 139
Colpi, Henri 142
Condamné à Mort s'est Échappé, Un 35, 37, 40, 41, 42–3, 44
Conrad, Joseph 179
Corbusier, Le 14
Cronaca di un Amore 125
Cumberland Story, The 72
Cybulski, Zbigniew 187

Dali, Salvador 18
Dames du Bois de Boulogne, Les 40
Dasté, Jean 29
Defeated People, A 71
De Gaulle, Charles 45, 148
De Lafayette, Madame 42, 148
Demy, Jacques 112, 185
De Sica, Vittorio 38, 123, 133
Devi 193, 195, 196, 197
Devigny, André 40, 45
Diary for Timothy, A 78–81
Dickens, Charles 17, 30, 125
Diderot, Denis 40
Dim Little Island 76
Dr Mabuse–the Gambler 87, 89–94, 100, 101, 116

Dr Strangelove 97
Dolce Vita, La 125–6, 127, 129, 131, 134
Donskoi, Mark 199
Dostoevsky, Fyodor 99, 125, 140
Douce 45
Dreyer, Carl 39, 167
Duras, Marguerite 142

Eclipse, The 143
Eight and a Half (8½) 121–2, 128, 129, 131, 132, 133
Einstein, Albert 187
Eisenstein, Sergei, 51–64, 171–2, 181, 187
Eisler, Hans 150
Eliot, T. S. 11, 39, 41, 113
Éluard, Paul 142
Empson, William 72, 133
Entertainer, The 75
Every Day except Christmas 75–6

Family Portrait 76
Fellini, Federico 30, 121–34
Feydeau, Georges 185
Franju, Georges 144
Frankenheimer, John 92, 105
Freud, Sigmund 60, 74, 130
Films and Filming 172
Fires were Started, The 76
First Days, The 67–8
Fitzgerald, Scott 131
Flanagan & Allen 69
Ford, Ford Madox 25
Forster, E. M. 78–9, 191, 198
Fury 98

Gabor, Zsa Zsa 163
Garbo, Greta 167

210

Garland, Judy 143, 163
Generale delle Rovere, Il 179
Generation, A 172, 176–9, 181, 187
George IV 191
Giacometti, Alberto 13
Gielgud, John 81
Gilbert, Maria Dolores 162
Gish, Lilian 11
Godard, Jean-Luc 25, 46, 112, 141, 167, 182
Goebbels 96, 104
Goethe, J. W. 89, 149
Gorki, Maxim 199
Gray, Thomas 72
Green, Henry 78
Grierson, John 68
Griffith, D. W. 11, 53, 95
Guernica 142

Hawks, Howard 141
Hegel, G. F. W. 24
Heir to Genghis Khan, The 53
Henri VI 127
Henze, Hans Werner 155
Hess, Myra 69, 79
Hiroshima Mon Amour 139, 140, 148–9
Himmler 149
Hitchcock, Alfred 104, 141, 183
Hitler 51–2, 85, 96–7
Honour, Hugh 191n
Hôtel des Invalides 144
Houston, Penelope 143
Huxley, Aldous 164
Huysmans, J.-K. 91

Innocent Sorcerers 173, 186, 187
Intolerance 53

In Which We Serve 68
It Happened Here 70
Ivan the Terrible 55, 63, 171–2, 175

Jalsaghar 196
James, Henry 125, 138
Jaubert, Maurice 23
Jennings, Humphrey 64, 67–81
Jones, Ernest 130
Journal d'un Curé de Campagne 36, 39, 42–3, 45
Jules et Jim 161–2
Justinian 147

Kachenjunga 193, 194, 195
Kael, Pauline 149
Kafka, Franz 109, 141
Kanal 177, 179, 182
Kelly, George 150–1
Kino-Phot 53
Kipling, Rudyard 191
Kerensky, Alexander 59
Klein Rogge, Rudolf 90, 97
Knight, Castleton 76
Kokoschka, Oskar 29
Kracauer, Siegfried 86–7, 100–01
Kropotkin, Prince 25
Kubrick, Stanley 97, 104
Kürsten, Peter 97

Lang, Fritz 55, 85–105, 109, 113, 115–16, 164
Lapoujade, Robert 56
Lassalle, Martin 38
Lattuada, Alberto 130
Lawrence, D. H. 126–7
Laydu, Claude 45
Leenhardt, Roger 142

Lehar, Franz 159
Lenin 59, 60
Léon Morin, prêtre 45
Leonardo 54, 57, 60, 62
Leskov, Nicolai 175–6
Letter from an Unknown Woman 160
Lewis, Wyndham 125
Leyda, Jay 53n
Listen to Britain 67, 68–9, 74, 80
Liszt, Franz 162
Lloyd, Harold 94
Lola 185
Lola Montès 162–8
Lomnicki, Tadeuz 187
London Can Take It 68
Lorre, Peter 98
Losey, Joseph 105
Lotna 174–5, 176, 186
Louis II 162, 166, 168
Louis XIV 148
Love at Twenty 186–7
Luci di Varietà 130
Lully 37
Lumière, Louis 123

'M'/*Murderer Amongst Us* 85, 87, 89, 92, 97–101, 110, 116
Madge, Charles 72–3
Magnificent Ambersons, The 143
Magritte, René 68
Mahanagar 193, 194, 195, 197
Maison Tellier, La 166
Mallarmé, Stéphane 144–5
Manchurian Candidate, The 92
Manet, Edouard 165
Marker, Chris 141, 148
Marquet, Jean-Paul 28
Marx, Karl 60, 141

Mason, James 161
McCarthy, Mary 151
McCarthy, Senator 111
Melville, Jean-Pierre 45
Metropolis 89, 92, 94–7, 100, 115
Meyerhold Vsevolod 58
Milne, A. A. 166
Milosz, Czeslaw 171
Modern Times 95
Modigliani, Amedeo 112
Mollo, Andrew 70
Montherlant, Henry de 45
Moore, Marianne 36, 38
Moraldo in Città 129
Mozart, W.A. 40, 44, 69
Müde Tod, Der 87, 91
Munk, Andrzej 150
Muriel 110, 139, 140–1, 150–5
Murnau, F. W. 91

Naipaul, V. S. 191–2
Napoleon 76, 90
Nelson 76
Night and Fog 149–50
Night Mail 73
Norwid, Cyprion 186
Nosferatu 91

October 54–5, 59, 60, 61, 62
Ophuls, Max 39, 159–68
Origen 129
Orphée 104
Osborne, John 75
Ostrovsky, Alexander 58
Ô Saisons, Ô Chateaux 148
Ozu, Yasujiro 47

Paris Nous Appartient 109–17, 140

Pasolini, Pier Paolo 172
Passenger 150
Passion de Jean D'Arc, La 39, 167
Pather Panchali 112–95, 197–201, 202, 204
Pavlov 56
Pearson, Gabriel 46n, 115–16
Péguy, Charles 115
Picasso, Pablo 142
Pickpocket 37, 38, 42–3
Pinter, Harold 76
Pirandello, Luigi 161
Piranesi, G.–B. 164
Plaisir, Le 166
Polo, Marco 191n.
Pound, Ezra 10, 54
Powell, Dilys 73
Praz, Mario 147
Procès de Jeanne D'Arc 39–40, 44
Proust, Marcel 122
Public Enemy 86
Pudovkin, V. I. 53

Quatre Cents Coups, Les 24, 31, 162
Queen Kelly 160
Que Viva Mexico 57

Rabindranath Tagore 193
Racine, Jean 40, 41, 144
Raine, Kathleen 72, 74
Raleigh, Walter 77
Ray, Satyajit 191–205
Rear Window 183
Redgrave, Michael 79
Red Desert, The 143
Reed, Carol 104
Rendezvous at Midnight 142
Renoir, Jean 161, 193, 198

Resnais, Alain 110, 137–55
Richards, I. A. 72
Riefenstahl, Leni 51–3, 56
River, The 198
Rivette, Jaques 105, 109–17
Robbe-Grillet, Alain 47, 142, 145–6
Roma, Città Aperta 124
Ronde, La 160, 166
Rosi, Francesco 58–9
Rossellini, Roberto 124, 179
Roud, Richard 141
Russian Miracle, The 60

Salès Gomès, P. E. 19–20
Salvatore Giuliano 58–9
Samson 179–80, 181
Sansom, William 76, 78
Sartre, Jean-Paul 27, 56, 152
Scarface 86
Scarlet Street 98
Schnitzler, Arthur 159
Sémolué, Jean 40
Seton, Marie 57, 60
Seven Days in May 92
Shakespeare, William 74, 77, 81, 112–14, 117, 126, 168, 175, 184
Shoeshine 123
Siberian Lady Macbeth 175–6, 186
Siegfried 95, 97
Sight and Sound 46, 76, 141, 149
Silent Village, The 70
Simon, Michel 25
Southerner, The 198
Spare Time 75
Spengler, Oswald 87–8, 94, 116
Spiders, The 89
Spione 87
Spring Offensive 78

Index

S.S. *Ionian* 76
Stalin, J. V. 51
Storm over Asia 53
Stokes, Adrian 14
Stonier, George 73
Strada, La 125, 128, 132
Strike 61, 63
Survey, 12 May 1937 73–4

Taylor, John Russell 144
Terra Trema, La 124
Testament of Dr Mabuse, The 86, 89, 101–4
Theodora 147
Third Man, The 104
Thorndike, Andrew & Annelie 60
Tolstoy, Leo 125
Toute la Mémoire du Monde 144
Trevor-Roper, Hugh 85
Trinon, Hadelin 184
Triumph of the Will 51–3
Truffaut, Francois 24, 30, 141, 161–2, 167
Two Daughters 193, 194

Ustinov, Peter 163, 166–7

Valentino, Rudolfo 52
Valéry, Paul 38, 147–8
Valorba, Franco 124
Varda, Agnès 141, 148
Verdi, Giuseppe 133
Veronese, Paolo 165
Victoria, Queen 90
Vidor, King 183, 184

Vierny, Sacha 142
Vigo, Jean 12, 17–31, 35
Visconti, Luchino 63, 124, 140
Vitelloni I 30, 128
Voglino, Bruno 20
Von Harbou, Thea 83, 89, 90, 91, 104
Von Stroheim, Erich 160

Wagner, Richard 103–4, 159
Wajda, Andrzej 12, 77, 105, 133, 171–87
Walbrook, Anton 159
Waugh, Evelyn 45, 78
Wedding March, The 160
Welles, Orson 39, 101, 123, 137–9, 141, 143, 144, 153, 155, 164, 166
Wells, H. G. 96
Werner, Oskar 162
White Nights 140
White Sheikh, The 130–1
Wilde, Oscar 60, 122
Wilder, Billy 160
Williams, Tennessee 61
Wilson, Angus 90
World of Apu, The see *Apu Sansar*
Woolf, Virginia 75, 154
Wright, Basil 73

Yeats W. B. 116, 146–7

Zavattini, Cesare 123, 124, 133
Zéro de Conduite 17–18, 22–4, 25, 29, 35
Zola, Emile 124